Small Water Enterprises in Africa
3: Sudan

Small Water Enterprises in Africa 3: Sudan

A study of small water enterprises in Khartoum

Mohamed Elamin Abdel Gadir

Series Editors: Cyrus Njiru and Mike Smith

Water, Engineering and Development Centre
Loughborough University
2006

Water, Engineering and Development Centre,
Loughborough University,
Leicestershire, LE11 3TU, UK

© WEDC, Loughborough University, 2006

ISBN 13 Paperback: 978 1 84380 096 5
ISBN Ebook: 9781788533539
Book DOI: http://dx.doi.org/10.3362/9781788533539

A catalogue record for this book is available from the British Library.

A reference copy of this publication is also available online at:
http://www.lboro.ac.uk/wedc/publications/

Gadir, M. E. A. (2006)
Small Water Enterprises in Africa 3: Sudan
A study of small water enterprises in Khartoum

WEDC (The Water, Engineering and Development Centre) at Loughborough University in the UK is one of the world's leading institutions concerned with education, training, research and consultancy for the planning, provision and management of physical infrastructure for development in low- and middleincome countries.

This edition is reprinted and distributed by Practical Action Publishing.
Since 1974, Practical Action Publishing has published and disseminated books and information in support of international development work throughout the world. Practical Action Publishing trades only in support of its parent charity objectives and any profits are covenanted back to Practical Action (Charity Reg. No. 247257, Group VAT Registration No. 880 9924 76).

All reasonable precautions have been taken by the WEDC, Loughborough University to verify the information contained in this publication. However, WEDC, Loughborough University does not necessarily endorse the technologies presented in this document. The published material is being distributed without warranty of any kind, either expressed or implied. The responsibility for the interpretation and use of the material lies with the reader. In no event shall the WEDC, Loughborough University be liable for damages as a result of their use.

This document is an output from a project funded by the UK
Department for International Development (DFID)
for the benefit of low-income countries.
The views expressed are not necessarily those of DFID.

Designed at WEDC by Kay Davey and Glenda McMahon
Front cover photo montage by Rod Shaw
Front cover photographs by Cyrus Njiru
Illustrations by Ken Chatterton

Acknowledgements

The editors wish to express gratitude to the in-country study team, consisting of Mohamed Elamin Abdel Gadir and Al Tayeb Yagoub, who undertook the work on behalf of ITDG.

The editors also wish to thank members of the UK research team comprising Mike Albu, Diana Mitlin and Gordon McGranahan, for their important role in the research project; and also to Mike Albu for his editorial contributions.

Contents

List of figures viii
List of tables viii
Acronyms ix

Executive Summary 1
Introduction 1
Water supply – The national context 2
Water supply in Greater Khartoum City 2
Informal urban settlements 3
Research location selection 4
Water services and poverty 4
Small water enterprises (SWEs) 5
Consumer perspectives on SWEs 6
Utility and official perspectives on SWEs 6

Chapter 1 8
Introduction
1.1   Background 8
1.1   Goal, purpose and outputs of the study 8
1.3   The study team 9
1.4   Structure of this report 10

Chapter 2 11
Water Supply in Sudan – The National Context
2.1   National water institutions 12
2.2   National Water Corporation 13
2.3   State Water Corporations 15

Chapter 3 16
Water Supply in Khartoum City
3.1   Brief history 16
3.2   Institutional arrangements 18
3.3   Legal regulatory framework 19
3.4   Water infrastructure 21
3.5   Water supplies and distribution 22
3.6   Water coverage and demand 23
3.7   Greater Khartoum City sub-sector map 25
3.8   Current water policy issues 25

Chapter 4.. **30**
Informal Urban Settlements in Khartoum
4.1   Informal settlements overview 30
4.2   Water services in informal settlements 32
4.3   Location selection 34

Chapter 5.. **36**
Water Services and Poverty
5.1   Methodology 36
5.2   Household income and water expenditure 36
5.4   Coping strategies... 44

Chapter 6.. **45**
Small Water Enterprises (SWEs)
6.1   Methodology 45
6.2   Overview of SWEs 45
6.3   Settlement sub-sector map 49
6.4   Value chain.. 50
6.5   Livelihoods of SWE operators 50
6.6   SWOT analysis 54

Chapter 7.. **56**
Consumer Perspectives on SWEs
7.1   Methodology 56
7.2   Information obtained... 56

Chapter 8.. **58**
Utility Perspectives on SWEs
8.1   Methodology 58
8.2   Official perspectives on SWEs 59

Chapter 9.. **61**
Consciousness Building

References **64**

List of figures

Breakdown of water costs for customers of water-cart vendors in
peri-urban settlements around Khartoum, Sudan...5
Figure 3.1. Map of Sudan 17
Figure 3.2. Map of Greater Khartoum.. 18
Figure 3.1. Greater Khartoum City sub-sector map................................ 25
Figure 4.1. Options for water services in informal settlements 32
Figure 6.1. Relationships between different stakeholders in the informal
            settlements in Khartoum State 46
Figure 6.2. Settlement sub-sector map 49
Figure 6.3. Breakdown of water costs for customers of water cart vendors
            in peri-urban settlements around Khartoum, Sudan 50

List of tables

Table 2.1. Sudan's existing and potential water resources (1999)............... 11
Table 2.2. The governance structure of water supply in Sudan.................... 12
Table 2.3. New institutional arrangements for water supply in Sudan........... 14
Table 2.4. Planned development and rehabilitation of water resources ....
            (2002–06)... 14
Table 3.1. Advantages and disadvantages of management options 27
Table 4.1. Summary of types of informal settlement in Khartoum 40
Table 5.1. Rough breakdown of household budgets................................. 41
Table 5.2. Average household water consumption for Dar Al Salam
            (Umm Durman) 41
Table 5.3. Household water consumption in April 2002 43
Table 6.1. Water revenue and expenditure from four water-yards
            in Omdurman town.. 47
Table 6.2. SWOT analysis 55
Table 8.1. Root causes of poor access to water and potential solutions........ 58
Table 9.1. Outcome of problem analysis. Problems faced by consumers....... 61
Table 9.2. Outcome of problem analysis. Problems as seen by vendors 62
Table 9.3. Outcome of problem analysis. Constraints as seen by KSWC........ 62

Acronyms

ADRA	Adventist Development and Relief Agency
ACF	Action Contre la Faim
AU	Administrative Unit
CBO	Community-Based Organization
Dawa	Al-Dawa Al-Islamiya
DFID	Department for International Development
HH	Household
IDP	Internally displaced people
IDPM	Institute for Development Policy and Management
IIED	International Institute for Environment and Development
ITDG	Practical Action (formerly the Intermediate Technology Development Group)
KSWC	Khartoum State Water Corporation
MSF	Médecins sans Frontières
NGO	Non-government organization
NWC	National Water Corporation
PC	Popular Committees
PPP	Private–public partnerships
PPPU	Ministry of Physical Planning & Public Utilities
PSP	Private sector participation
RWC	Rural Water Corporation (pre-1994)
SD	Sudan Dinar
SWC	State Water Corporation
SWE	Small water enterprise
UPAP	Urban Upgrading and Poverty Alleviation Project
UWC	Urban Water Corporation (pre-1994)
WEDC	Water, Engineering and Development Centre, Loughborough University
WHO	World Health Organization

Executive Summary

Introduction

This report is part of an action-research project by WEDC, ITDG (now Practical Action) and WaterAid about improving access to water in informal urban settlements. It focuses on Khartoum in Sudan, one of four African cities selected for study.

The research aims to improve the well-being of the poor in informal urban settlements through cost-effective improved water supply services. It focuses on small-scale private-sector providers and vendors of water – referred to as small water enterprises (or SWEs). It seeks to develop practical methods of enabling SWEs, in partnership with water utilities, to play a more effective role in the provision of water.

The first phase of the research, as reported here, was intended to develop a contextual understanding of SWEs in each city; sensitize the action-researchers to critical aspects of the operation of SWEs; build contacts and consensus within the utilities and other relevant agencies; and identify, assess and select interventions to improve SWE performance for the Phase 2.

The key research questions for Phase 1 were:

1. How do different groups of poor people in urban informal settlements currently obtain access to water services and what are their (major) remaining needs?

2. What incentives and constraints exist for SWEs to improve the water services they provide to the poor?

3. What constraints exist (and what opportunities might exist) for utilities to engage with SWEs to improve services to users within informal urban settlements?

4. What are the key obstacles that block collaboration between utilities and SWEs in informal urban settlements, and how might they be overcome?

5. What are appropriate improvements to service standards and how can they be secured?

6. How can others benefit from the lessons learned from successful interventions to improve services to users?

Water supply – The national context

The Republic of Sudan has a federal structure with both a national and 26 state governments. The National Water Corporation (NWC) – under the Ministry of Irrigation and Water Resources – is responsible for national water resource development policy, national research, the specification of water and infrastructure standards, the training of a technical cadre, and providing guidelines to state authorities.

The State Water Corporations – under the Ministry of Physical Planning and Public Utilities – are responsible for the operation and maintenance of the water supply facilities, execution of approved national (NWC) projects, and implementation of local projects funded by the state's budget.

National planning is focused on the rehabilitation of existing water supply systems and investment in new water resources – particularly Nile water extraction plants in Khartoum. National policy is to encourage the private sector to invest in water supplies in both rural and urban areas countrywide.

Water supply in Greater Khartoum City

Greater Khartoum, comprising the 'three cities' of Umm Durman, Al Khurtum and Al Khartoum Bahri, straddles the confluence of the Blue and White Niles. The older residential areas, close to the river, were originally well-served by Khartoum State Water Corporation's (KSWC) network, which was built in the 1950s to treat and distribute water from the Nile.

In the last 20 years, however, the population of the city has roughly trebled. The network serving formal residential areas has become dilapidated, over-loaded and misused. Meanwhile, a vast geographical area of 'informal' settlements has grown up around the original three cities. They are unserved by the piped network – but home to around 4 million migrants and internally displaced people.

The informal settlements – extending up to 40km from the Nile – rely on groundwater extracted from shallow and deep aquifers. The principal extraction points are 'water-yard' boreholes and wells, where water is stored in large elevated tanks and sold to surrounding households via SWEs – mainly vendors using donkey-drawn water carts. There are around 900 such water-yards (also called water supply stations) around Khartoum. Most were established by emergency relief non-government organizations (NGOs) during successive waves of migration / displacement – but as the NGOs withdrew, most have been taken over by KSWC.

The water-yards, and the SWEs that serve them, supply the bulk of water in Khartoum (estimated at 300,000 m³/day, compared to the KSWC Nile water treatment plants that produce 260,000 m³/day). At least two-thirds of the population of greater Khartoum relies on these water-yards.

KSWC's planning priorities focus on rehabilitating the existing piped network and expanding the capacity of the Nile water extraction and treatment plant. Since the existing network serves only 210,000 households, this offers little prospect of improved access to water for the millions living outside formal urban residential areas.

Although water tariffs for network customers are historically low and heavily subsidized, since 1991 KSWC has tried to ensure that the water-yards were financially self-reliant. This enabled KSWC to begin experimenting in 2002 with alternative management arrangements – including community participation through 'Popular Committees' and private-sector management.

In particular, Water Management Committees were established by KSWC with local community representatives to supervise water-yard facilities, collect water revenues, and pay for maintenance. These committees do not operate well, however, nor do they genuinely engage the local community. Also, KSWC lacks sufficient competent engineers to maintain all the water-yards efficiently. As a result, most water-yards remain dilapidated and unreliable – suffering frequent breakdowns and inefficiencies – with negative impact on both SWEs and their customers.

Informal urban settlements

Khartoum's informal urban settlements are unique in form and history. They were constructed very rapidly on desert land surrounding the original 'three cities' to accommodate great waves of internal refugees and migrants fleeing drought and civil war during the 1980s and 1990s.

They now house around 4 million people in extremely harsh conditions. Homes are constructed of adobe (mud bricks), plastic sheets and corrugated tin. The landscape is entirely barren. Most of the year it is extremely hot (40°C+) and there is negligible rainfall. Poverty is intense. Infrastructure, health and education services are very poor or entirely absent.

Water services are critical to quality of life in the settlements, including the ability to construct shelter, since water is essential for brick-making. Water-yards are the principal source of water for 95 per cent of the population, alongside old irrigation wells and handpumps in some locations.

The official status of the settlements varies. 'Spontaneous' areas are liable to arbitrary demolition. Other former camps of displaced people have a degree of recognition. Official interest in formalizing the settlements is growing – with plans for roads and electricity services being implemented in some areas.

Research location selection

Research was conducted in two districts:

- **Soba Al Aradi** (on the southern periphery of Al Khartoum)

- **Dar Al Salam** (on the western periphery of Umm Durman)

The locations were selected for research on the basis that they have planning department recognition, are not liable to demolition, feature high poverty levels and poor services, and are very unlikely to be connected to piped water in the near future. Both locations rely on water-yards for supplies and the majority of households are served by water vendors.

Water services and poverty

Research revealed that households average seven people. Unskilled labour on farms and in the city is the main occupation. Some 90 per cent of households have an average income of less than SD20,000 (US$80) per month. Most reported taking only one or two meals a day of sorghum (dura), with beans, oil, sugar and seasonal vegetables a luxury. Travel costs, charcoal for cooking, water, and education take up a large part of household income.

In the poorest areas, households spend between 17 and 25 per cent of their income on water for domestic use (typically SD4000 (US$15) per month to purchase 125–170 litres/day). Proximity to a water-yard enables direct collection, especially by children, who do not have to pay for small quantities. Water costs are very sensitive to water-yard performance. The breakdown of a local water-yard has immediate and very significant impacts on prices charged by vendors (increases of 150 per cent were reported), as well as removing the option of direct water collection.

Households cope with this by limiting consumption (by as much as half), and also by resorting to low-grade water sources such as old irrigation canals and saline wells.

The other major water use in informal settlements is for construction (brick-making) and to a lesser extent small businesses such as restaurants, tea sellers, local beer makers and small dairy farms.

Small water enterprises (SWEs)

The principal water supply system in the informal settlements is water vendors using the water-yard and donkey carts. At the water-yards, submersible pumps draw borehole water up from 100–200 metres into an elevated tank. This serves large-volume standpipes from which the donkey carts are filled. The carts deliver water to 95 per cent of homes, selling water by the jerrycan. In around 5 per cent of households women and children also collect water directly from water-yards.

Research indicates that around 30–40,000 donkey cart water vendors operate throughout Khartoum. Most are young men or boys (age 12–35), and many are the main breadwinner for their households. Most own their own carts, but renting from a cart-owner for a fixed fee or a share of income is also common. Their income is not very different from the rest of the settlement to which they belong. Typical vendor earnings range from SD400–1000 (US$2–5) per day.

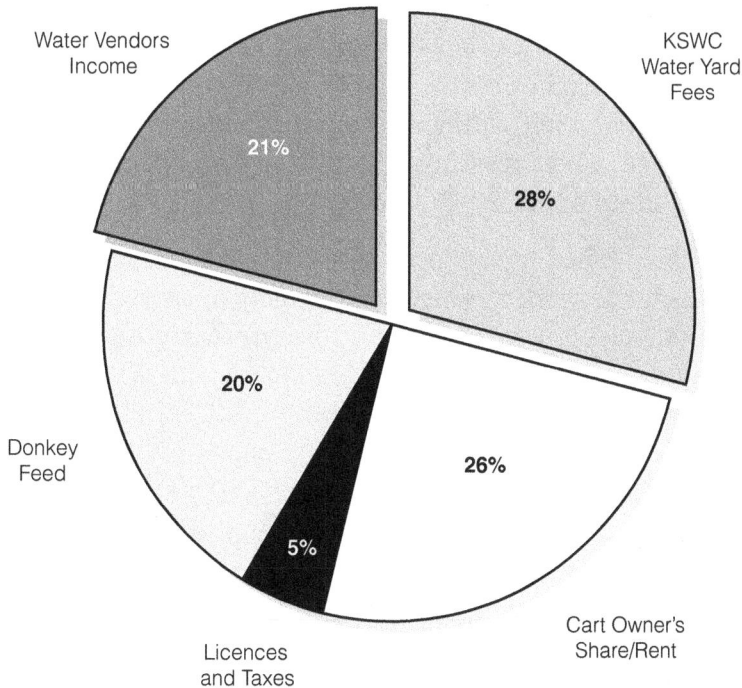

Water Vendors
Income

KSWC
Water Yard
Fees

21%

28%

20%

26%

Donkey
Feed

5%

Cart Owner's
Share/Rent

Licences
and Taxes

Breakdown of water costs for customers of water-cart vendors in peri-urban settlements around Khartoum, Sudan

The economics of the typical water-yard – donkey cart system are not efficient.

KSWC water-yards charge vendors around SD0.2 per litre (SD70 for a cartload) – regardless of whether they work for an NGO or are private operators. Households, however, pay SD0.7–1 per litre. Most of the mark-up is accounted for by haulage costs, such as cart hire and donkey feed.

This helps explain why consumer prices rise so steeply when water-yards break down (a weekly occurrence in some areas) and cart operators have to travel further afield for water.

Substantial delays were observed at water-yards – with dozens of carts waiting long periods to collect water in disorganized, inefficient and at times unhygienic conditions. There is significant scope for reducing consumers' costs by improving water-yard layout and operations to help cart operators.

A raft of five separate annual licences and taxes raised on cart operators by the Ministry of Health and local municipal authorities adds to the cost of delivering water, creates major opportunities for rent-seeking by officials, and causes further inefficiency as cart-operators try to evade their attention.

Consumer perspectives on SWEs

Water users share concerns about poor water-yard performance and the effect this has on water services and prices. Generally, consumers view cart operators in a positive light – noting their willingness to fetch water from more distant yards when necessary and, where relationships were well established, to provide water on credit during times of financial difficulty.

Some households wished to see local piped networks running from their local water-yards. Such a network was installed privately in one block in Dar Al Salam. However, even though it was significantly cheaper than water vendors, residents objected to paying a rate that was three times more than the (highly subsidized) rate paid by those with access to KSWC's central Khartoum mains network.

Utility and official perspectives on SWEs

When the problems of water services in informal settlements were discussed with KSWC and government officers, typically these officials identify inadequate water treatment plant and deficiencies in the mains piped network. Attention and resources are given to plans to install a new large-scale Nile water extraction and treatment plant, and to rehabilitate the mains network. Water-yards are seen as a necessary temporary solution, and the role of vendors (such as donkey cart operators) is rarely acknowledged.

KSWC rural water manager Al Tayeb Yagoub said 'Only after being part of this research did I start to realize the importance of vendors and the role they play in water distribution to households. Now in my fieldwork I am attracted by the vendors as key partners.'

Chapter 1

Introduction

1.1   Background

This report is part of wider research about 'Better Access to Water in Informal Urban Settlements through Support to Small Water-Providing Enterprises', which was financed by the UK Department for International Development's (DFID) Engineering Knowledge and Research programme (EngKAR). Four African cities were selected for study: Accra in Ghana, Nairobi in Kenya, Dar es Salaam in Tanzania, and Khartoum in Sudan.

1.1   Goal, purpose and outputs of the study

The **goal** of the research is *to raise the well being of the poor in informal urban settlements through cost-effective improved water supply services.*

Its **purpose** is *to identify and test constraints, opportunities and strategies for enabling small-scale independent providers to deliver acceptable water service to poor urban consumers.*

Study focus, aims and objectives

The focus of the study was provision of water in un-served or inadequately served low-income urban settlements where conventional water supply is very limited. It focuses on small-scale private-sector providers of water – referred to here as small water enterprises (or SWEs). The research aims to build on available knowledge of SWEs so as to develop practical methods of enabling them to play a more effective part in the provision of water in informal urban settlements, in partnership with water utilities. The research also investigated what market incentives exist for better water services, and how these can be realized.

The research is divided into two phases.

Phase 1 was intended to:
• Analyse the operating environment and develop a contextual understanding of SWEs in Khartoum and the three other cities.

- Sensitize the researchers to critical aspects of the operation of SWEs.

- Build contacts within the utilities and other relevant agencies.

- Identify, assess and select Phase 2 interventions to improve the performance of SWEs.

Phase 2 will conduct action research to pilot, develop and implement at least two of the interventions assessed as being the most likely to succeed. These interventions will seek to improve water services for the urban poor who rely on SWEs for delivery of water.

Key research issues

Drawing from the goal, purpose and the contextual understanding developed in the Inception Phase, the following overarching research issues were identified for Phase 1:

1. How do different groups of poor people in urban informal settlements currently obtain access to water services and what are their (major) remaining needs?

2. What incentives and constraints exist for SWEs to improve the water services they provide to the poor?

3. What constraints exist (and what opportunities might exist) for utilities to engage with SWEs to improve services to users within informal urban settlements?

4. What are key obstacles that block collaboration between utilities and SWEs in informal urban settlements, and how might they be overcome?

5. What are appropriate improvements to service standards and how can they be secured?

6. How can others benefit from the lessons learned from successful interventions to improve services to users?

1.3   The study team

The Sudanese research team comprised:
Mohamed Elamin Abdel Gadi – Social Researcher
Al Tayeb Yagoub – Water Utility Engineer

The UK-based support team comprised:
Mike Smith, Project/Programme Manager, WEDC
Cyrus Njiru, Research Manager/Principal Researcher, WEDC

Mike Albu, Enterprise Development Specialist, ITDG
Diana Mitlin, Social Development Specialist, IIED/IDPM
Gordon McGranahan, Development Economist, IIED

1.4   Structure of this report

The report presents the key findings about how to improve access to water in informal urban settlements by supporting small water enterprises.

Chapter 2 puts the national water supply in context. It outlines the main water resources available, national institutional arrangements, and major changes under way.

Chapter 3 focuses on the water supply situation in Khartoum and it covers the institutional reforms underway and administrative arrangements in place at different levels of local government; water supply coverage and demand; existing water supply sources and infrastructure; the legal and regulatory framework; and a city-level sub-sector map that summarizes the information from this section.

Chapter 4 is an overview of the types and significance of informal urban poor settlements in Khartoum and the different forms of water supply services in the settlements. The criteria used for selecting the research locations is discussed in this chapter.

Chapter 5 focuses on the relationship between water and household poverty in the study area. It explains how inadequate access to water services impacts on poverty and how poverty influences access to water services.

Chapter 6 describes the structure, role and function of SWEs. It also explains the livelihoods of those who work in them, the forces that govern their working practices, their perceived constraints and their hopes for improvement.

Chapter 7 provides consumer perspectives on water services provided by SWEs.

Chapter 8 illustrates the attitudes of government officials and water utility staff towards the goal of improving access to water in informal settlements, and the role that SWEs could play in achieving that goal.

Chapter 9 describes stakeholders' conclusions about feasible and effective ways to improve access to water in informal settlements.

Finally, recommendations for Phase 2 action research are given in Chapter 10.

Chapter 2

Water Supply in Sudan – The National Context

The water supply systems throughout the country include water-yards (boreholes fitted with tanks), boreholes, handpumps, private treatment plants (mostly on the Nile), check dams, shallow wells, open reservoirs, permanent and seasonal rivers, and others. The type of water supply system used depends on the location.

In 1999 existing and potential water resources in Sudan were estimated as follows:

Table 2.1. Sudan's existing and potential water resources (1999)		
Water resources	**Capacity (billion m³/year)**	**Constraints**
Current Nile extraction	20.5	Seasonal pattern coupled with limited storage
Non-Nile rivers and streams	5.4	Highly variable, short duration flow, difficult to monitor or harvest
Renewable groundwater extraction	4.1	Deep water, entailing high pumping costs Remote areas with weak infrastructure
Current total	**30.0**	
Expected share from reclamation of swamps	6.0	Capital intensive with considerable social and environmental cost
Total	**36.0**	

Source: NWC, 1999

2.1 National water institutions

Until 1994, responsibility for water resources and supply was divided between two national state institutions, the Rural Water Corporation (RWC) and the Urban Water Corporation (UWC). Water research and services was the mandate of the Rural Water Corporation, which had two main departments: Groundwater and Surface Water.

In 1994 the two corporations were amalgamated into the National Water Corporation (NWC). This coincided with the implementation of a federal system of government and the creation of 26 states. Within each state, water services and resource management were delegated to a State Water Corporation.

Table 2.2. The governance structure of water supply in Sudan			
Governance level		**Key institutions**	**Key people**
National	Sudan is a national federation of 26 semi-autonomous states.	Ministry of Irrigation and Water Resources National Water Corporation (NWC)	Minister for Irrigation and Water Resources NWC Director
Khartoum State	Each state has a governor (*Wali*), a cabinet of seven ministers, and an elected assembly. Khartoum State has the largest population – an estimated 7 million people.	Ministry of Physical Planning & Public Utilities (PPPU) Khartoum State Water Corporation (KSWC)	State Minister for PPPU State Minister for Health KSWC Director
Mahalia	Each state is divided up into 'local authorities' or *Mahalia*. Khartoum State has seven *Mahalia*.	Department of Health / Public Health Department	Commissioner (*Motamad*) Department of Health Directors
Administrative unit	Each *Mahalia* is divided into Administrative Units (AUs). There are 36 AUs in Khartoum State. Each AU typically governs about 45,000–70,000 people.	Public Health Unit	Public health inspectors
Local	Popular Committees (PC) – are partly political and partly administrative entities. There are 15–20 Popular Committees in each AU. In Khartoum, this means each PC is responsible for a 'block' of around 500 households.		Local PC Chairpersons

The National Water Corporation's mandate is to provide adequate water supplies for human and livestock consumption and for other purposes. Water for human consumption should comply with World Health Organization (WHO) guidelines and Ministry of Health standards.

Each state government is meant to operate and maintain water sources and finance their State Water Corporations. Meanwhile the federal government – through the National Water Corporation – allocates external funding to the state government.

The Local Governance Act directs each state to establish an autonomous State Drinking Water Corporation. This body is owned by the Ministry of Physical Planning and Public Utilities. Although the UWC and RWC were dissolved at the national level, they still exist at state level and work side by side as departments of the State Water Corporations. The most senior manager of the two departments, whether UWC or RWC, leads the State Drinking Water Corporation.

2.2   National Water Corporation

The National Water Corporation (NWC) is mandated to carry out the following functions at the central level:

- National policy formulation regarding water resource development and use

- Specification of water supply equipment and design of water facilities (using standard specifications)

- Training of technical staff at national level

- National projects allocation and execution

- Coordination at national, state and local authority levels

- Development of general guiding policies for water resource development countrywide

- Preparation of designs, specifications and tenders for work that will be put out to tender

National research departments are included within the Ground and Wadis Administration, which falls under the responsibility of the Ministry of Irrigation and Water Resources. The two production sections – Drilling and Construction – are included as sections within the National Company for Drilling and the National Company for Water Resource Development respectively.

Table 2.3.   New institutional arrangements for water supply in Sudan

New institutional arrangements	Former arrangements (Rural Water Corporation)
Ground & Wadis (Valleys) Administration (MolWR) Ground Water Research Meteorology and Surface Water Research	Ground Water Department Ground Water Research Drilling section
National Company for Drilling	Surface Water Department
National Company for Water Resource Development (construction of *hafirs* and dams)	Meteorology and Surface Water Research

For Khartoum, details of the National Water Plan for 2002–06 focus on rehabilitating the existing water supply systems and investing in establishing new water sources. The target for new supply is 567,000 m³, which is the estimated demand for 2006. This will cost about SD33.4 billion (US$130 million) according to the Social Information Unit of the Ministry of Finance. The national policy is to encourage the private sector to invest in water supply in both rural and urban areas countrywide.

The 2002–06 national plans provide for the development and rehabilitation of water resources as outlined in Table 2.4.

Table 2.4.   Planned development and rehabilitation of water resources (2002–06)

National water resource planning	Rehabilitation planned	New sources planned
Artesian wells (boreholes)	2009	602
Shallow wells (hand-dug wells)	1662	150
Handpumps	n.a.	1800
Reservoir *(hafirs)*	502	137
Check dams	15	89
Water treatment plants	97	0
Nile water stations	38	20

2.3   State Water Corporations

The State Water Corporations are financed by their respective state governments to operate and maintain water sources, while funding from the Central Government is allocated through the National Water Corporation. The NWC normally delegates the SWCs to supervise the execution of approved national projects, with the NWC providing support where necessary. The SWCs submit proposals to the NWC, prioritizing their needs and identifying locations.

The SWC's responsibilities are as follows:

- Operation and maintenance of water supply facilities

- Facility management (or delegation of management responsibility to an other body)

- Implementation of local projects funded by the state budget

In some cases the SWC is delegated powers by the NWC to execute national projects locally. In these cases salaries and budgets are designed and approved by the state authorities.

Chapter 3

Water Supply in Khartoum City

The capital of Khartoum State is sometimes referred to as 'Greater Khartoum' (see Figures 3.1 and 3.2). It is actually composed of three cities: Al Khartoum, Al Khartoum Bahri, and Umm Durman (Omdurman), which are separated by the Blue Nile and While Nile rivers. The three cities are well connected by bridges across the rivers.

3.1 Brief history

The ongoing civil war, long-term drought, tribal conflict and banditry have caused wide displacement of people all over the country. Most internally displaced people (IDPs) are from the Southern and Nuba ethnic groups and other Western tribes such as the Fur and Missiriya. Khartoum State has received the largest proportion of IDPs (about 50 per cent). Some 75 per cent of those who reached the capital between 1984 and 1992 were young people (less than 25 years old). According to Banaga (2002) Khartoum attracted the majority of IDPs because 75 per cent of industry and 56 per cent of services are in Khartoum, therefore most job opportunities are there; and there is easy access to international NGOs and humanitarian assistance. Also most IDPs have relatives in the capital that can be expected to provide them with moral and material support.

Urban and peri-urban areas that are not part of the piped network in Khartoum still tend to be labelled 'rural' by water utility officials – even though these settlements have relatively high population densities and minimal agriculture.

In the early 1970s, the population of Khartoum State (including the three cities Khartoum, Khartoum North and Omdurman and the surrounding area) was estimated at 2 million people. Most were served by piped water networks, bringing water from the Nile treatment plants. Following the second civil war (1983) and the 1984–5 droughts, the capital attracted about 1.8 million more people from the war and drought-affected areas. In addition records show that the state population over the last two decades (1985 to 2005) increased from 3.5 to 7 million people.

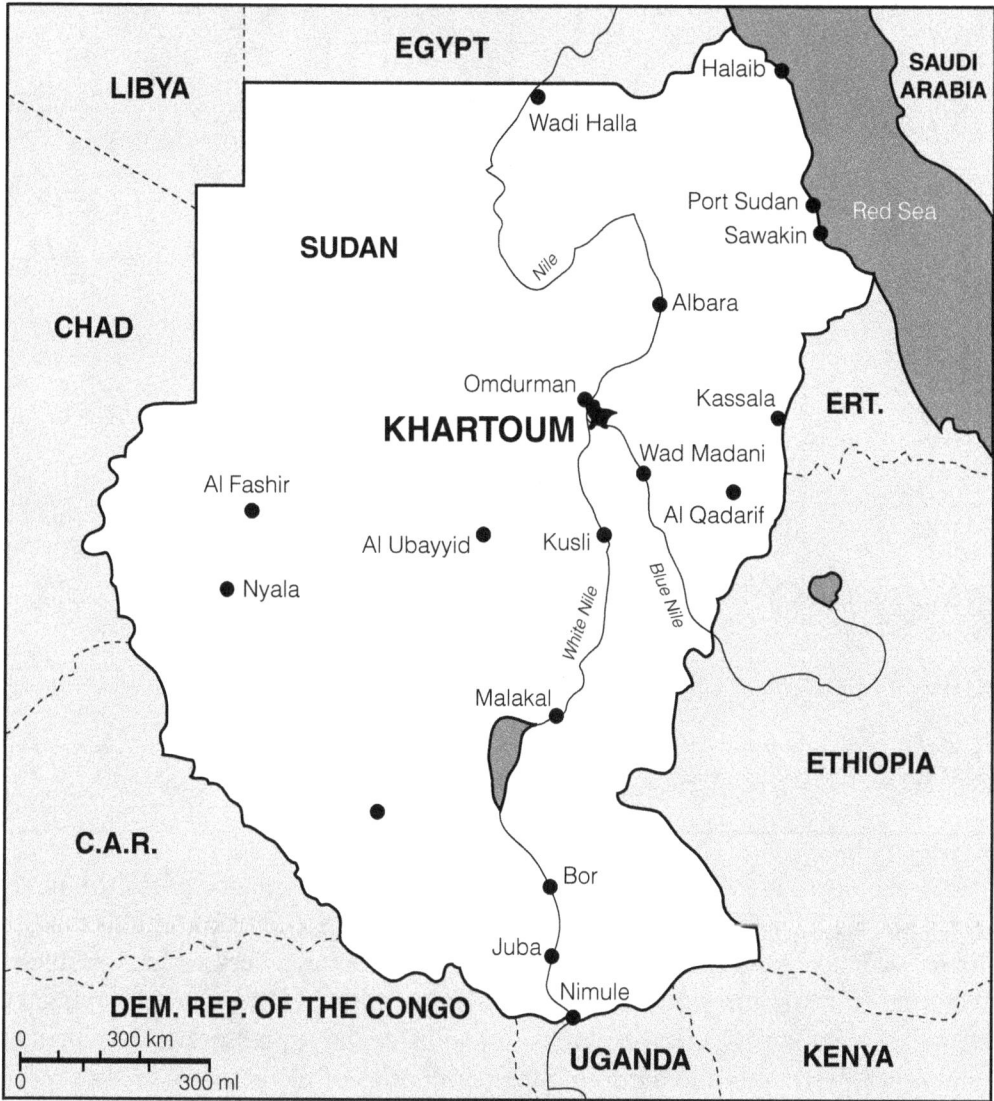

Figure 3.1. Map of Sudan

This aggravated the water situation, putting pressure on the water supply system and leading to exploitation of other water resources, mainly groundwater from deep aquifers.

The distribution networks are old, have low capacity and did not match the expansion of the settlements. The main water distribution lines are also very old (established in the 1950s) and their designed capacity is only 50 per cent that of the new pumping stations. When pipes need to be replaced, one metre of new pipe costs about US$10.

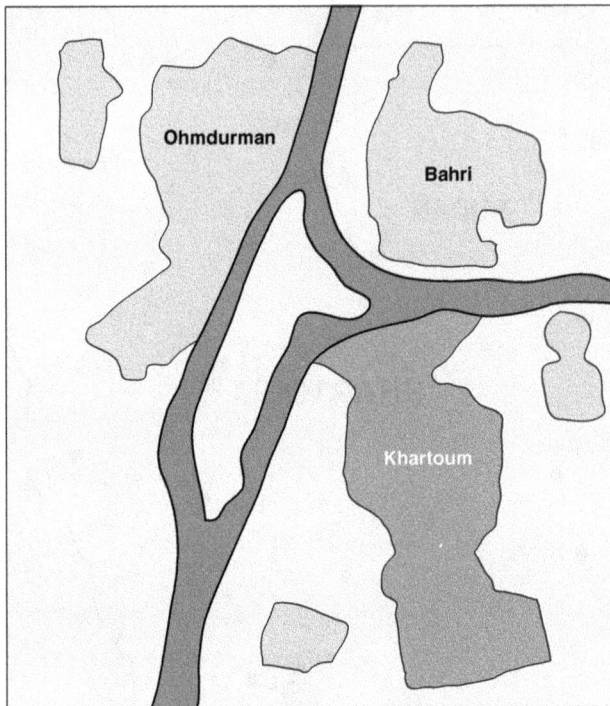

Figure 3.2. Map of Greater Khartoum

Water shortages are common in peripheral settlements connected to the piped networks. Excessive and uneconomic use of water by the few households that are directly connected to the water distribution networks is a very serious problem. Watering of lawns and gardens, for example, is common. Often water is extracted from the network using electric pumps – creating negative pressure in the pipelines (major health hazard) and depriving the peripheries of the network of supply.

The failure of the piped network distribution to serve individual households due to improper design, low pressure, and frequent breakdown means that the services of the water vendors are needed to augment the water shortages. The extent of this problem is not explicitly acknowledged by Khartoum State Water Corporation, however.

3.2 Institutional arrangements

The Khartoum State Water Corporation (KSWC) had two administrative units: the Urban Water Administration, which is concerned with urban areas directly connected to the main water supply network, and the Rural Water Administration, concerned with water provision to settlements outside the piped network who mainly rely on standpipes for their water supply.

The Rural Water Administration enjoyed UNICEF support, which opened ways to community participation and inclusion, and linked water with sanitation (which is also a merit of NGOs' interventions in poor areas such as informal IDPs settlements, including the Es Salam camps, Mayo farms, the Soba Al Aradi Al Salam Jebel Awlia and Al Takamul Idd Babikir Id Hessian settlements, and others). However the KSWC has been restructured and the Rural Water Administration was then merged into the Urban Water Corporation.

UNICEF supports the national Water and Environmental Sanitation programme that links hygienic water supply with environmental sanitation. NGOs also play an important role in the programmes in poorer settlements, e.g. Mayo Farm, Dar Al Salam Jebel Awlia, Idd Babikir, Wad Al Basheer, Dar Al Salam Omdurman, and many others.

The state authority decided that KSWC would be responsible for drilling and building water supply facilities and the local authority for managing them. But the local authorities did not have the experience to find and develop funding to replace the funds being withdrawn by the national government, and within a period of three or four years the facilities had deteriorated so much that the authorities had to appeal to the KSWC to rehabilitate them. This coincided with a withdrawal of NGOs, who had handed over management responsibilities to community development committees who had also failed to run them. Thus the KSWC began to retake management responsibilities, starting in Darushab, Umbadda West and Soug Lybia. The community development committees have also experienced difficulties in managing the water facilities, and have asked KSWC to resume responsibility for management of the water-yards once again.

3.3 Legal regulatory framework

The roles of the Khartoum State Water Corporation (KSWC) are to:

- provide adequate safe water for the state's urban and rural population;

- establish water resources;

- select suitable sites for new water supply facilities;

- decide on the best design for each facility;

- construct the water supply stations (or water-yards), which includes drilling, testing the water, and installing the station and the distribution system; and

- establish the water management systems.

Prior to 1990, water provision for human consumption for households not directly connected to piped networks was free in rural areas (water utilities are state enterprises). Water was considered a public good that should be provided free in a modern society by the state. The Rural Water Corporation paid for salaries, repairs and maintenance.

In 1991 the RWC endorsed the policy of self-reliance and the water tariff was invented. Popular Committees were to collaborate with the Khartoum State Water Corporation (KSWC), and thus Water Management Committees were established. In most cases the committees are composed of 12 representatives, including two from the local authority, three from Popular Committees, two local leaders, two from teacher's groups, one from women's groups, one youth representative, and one water-yard staff member.

The Water Management Committees' functions are to:

- supply fuel and lubricants;
- provide technical supervision and manage the water-yard;
- purchase spare parts for minor maintenance;
- pay for repairs and maintenance costs;
- collect water revenue directly from individual households; and
- submit weekly reports.

To enable them to accomplish these tasks training was extended to the Water Management Committees, including in mechanics, accounting, and community-based management of public utilities. Some NGOs – in collaboration with KSWC – carried out public health awareness education around water hygiene and environmental sanitation in communities without direct water connections.

Support for hygiene promotion as practised by NGOs like Action Contre la Faim (ACF) included:

- environmental hygiene education, including malaria prevention (measures to improve water drainage);
- ensuring that both vendors and consumers adopt better personal and environmental hygiene practices;
- promoting the need to build latrines and improve waste disposal;
- providing technical advice to build suitable latrines and ensure that they are used properly by all members of the family;

- providing information about the links between sanitation, hygiene and health; and

- providing information about the causes of water-borne diseases.

The water revenue that is collected is designed to meet operating costs and so to provide a steady water supply to all households covered by the facility. It is not explained to consumers, however, that they are paying not for the water but for the operating and maintenance costs. The Popular Committees (PCs) are managing the facilities on behalf of the community. Although there are representatives of the various sectors on the Water Management Committee, the links between consumer groups, the utility and local authorities are not institutionalized. This is important to encourage participation and engage the community in water supply and management. As it is now, consumers are passive recipients of the public service.

3.4   Water infrastructure

Khartoum state is endowed with great water resource potential, including the waters of the Nile and a groundwater aquifer. The three towns stretch along the Blue Nile, White Nile and the Great Nile, where there are six water treatment stations: Old Mugran, New Mugran, Burri, Old Bahri, New Bahri, and Omdurman. These water treatment stations are directly connected to residential areas, industrial areas, trade centres and institutions, but the service is not extended to most of the poor areas. The piped water distribution network covers 65 per cent of the urban areas of Khartoum State (UPAP, 2002).

Khartoum state has an annual rainfall of about 200 mm. There are 23 open water reservoirs (hafirs) where rainwater is collected, but that water is not safe for direct human consumption. The state has many good shallow wells, and there are 523 handpumps, mostly installed by NGOs in poor informal settlements. Water from handpumps is safe and could easily be protected against contamination by educating users on their proper use.

There are about 620 artesian wells, some of which augment the treatment plants that pump water from the Nile. Others are installed in the peripheries of the three towns. The overall state water deficit is estimated at 40 per cent. This deficit is more apparent in the peripheral areas and new extensions, where water is obtained from standpipes and distributed by water vendors using donkey carts.

The water deficit is a result of many factors: there is a lack of spare parts and repairs and maintenance are not regular; many water-yards run on electricity, which suffers from continual cuts; and there is low storage capacity, especially at the water-yards that serve the peripheral areas and new extensions.

In general, most water in the state is safe for human consumption, however the Nile water is contaminated during the flooding season (June–October), and some artesian wells suffer from bacterial infection caused by water runoff, which infiltrates through unsealed well tubes. Such contaminated wells are treated with chlorine. Other sources, such as hafirs and shallow wells, are hazardous. The handling of water by vendors and households can also lead to water contamination.

The state's water supply system includes six water treatment plants (or stations), 884 boreholes and standpipes, 612 handpumps, 2 small dams, 7 formal and about 120 local hafirs, and more than 200 open wells. The Khartoum State Water Corporation is entirely responsible for the state's drinking water supply.

The average daily water supply provided from treatment plants, boreholes, and other resources for both urban semi-urban and rural areas is:

Treatment plants	260,000 m³/day
Boreholes and others	350,000 m³/day
Total approximately	610,000 m³/day

3.5　Water supplies and distribution

In Khartoum State there are three means of water supply and distribution to households.

Urban zone

Here the distribution is by piped networks to household taps. The cost of water is low and services are accessible.

Semi-urban zone

This zone consists mainly of two categories of informal settlements: those that are not connected to the main water supply network, and poor informal settlements located in the peripheries and remote from the urban centre. These are the least-developed settlements and are characterized by poor infrastructure. The demand in this zone is very high because water is needed for building as well as other household needs. The vendors (donkey cart water sellers) play the central role in water distribution to these poor settlements, but their prices are high.

In big villages water is distributed through simple, old and poorly designed networks, most of them using donkeys and jerrycans for the final stage up to the households.

Most of the old settlement extensions and new settlements are on the outskirts of the city. They have come from rural areas, in particular non-arid areas where water conservation habits are uncommon, and have brought with them traditional behaviour that uses a lot of water and is not very sanitary in the conditions of a built-up area.

Water shortages are often attributed to breakdowns of reciprocating pumps in the water-yards that serve most rural populations.

3.6   Water coverage and demand

According to the official figures, the total daily water requirement for Khartoum state is about 1 million m³/day. This figure is based on the following demand assumptions:

(a)   The desirable per capita water consumption for an urban population is estimated at 180 litres per person per day. This makes 540,000 m³/day for Khartoum's 3 million people.

(b)   For the 4 million rural people unconnected to the piped network, daily per capita consumption is estimated at 70 litres per person per day, so total water demand is 280,000 m³/day.

(c)   Total human consumption (a + b) = 820,000 m³/day.

(d)   Water for other uses (industry, government institutions and public utilities) and network losses are estimated at 25 per cent of total human consumption (c above) = 205,000 m³/day.

(e)   Total demand (a + b + d) = 1,025,000 m³/day.

(f)   Present total daily supply = 657,000 m³/day.

(g)   Total daily deficit (e - f) = 370,000 m³/day.

This deficit is almost 36 per cent, which is not far off other estimates that put the deficit at 40 per cent.

The current daily water supply is provided by the following sources:

1.   Nile treatment plants   280,000 m³/day

2.   Water-yards   300,000 m³/day

3.   Handpumps   12,000 m³/day

4.   Other sources   65,000 m³/day
     (irrigation wells, irrigation open canals, hafirs)

5.   Total $(1 + 2 + 3 + 4) = 657,000 \text{ m}^3/\text{day}$

Sources: KSWC and senior management interviews (October 2003)

Note: About 90 per cent of households connected to water distribution networks lack storage tanks. Therefore in times of scarcity (during the dry season/summer) they use electric pumps, which are associated with a lot of waste.

To improve the water supply system a number of interrelated projects are planned, including the rehabilitation of the treatment plants (Khartoum North, Burri, Gamair, Khartoum Industrial area) and installation of new artesian wells. There are also plans to replace obsolete segments of the old distribution pipes, and to upgrade both the water testing facility and the capacity of water corporation projects. The plan's total budget is about US$4 million. The plan only covers water distribution through piped networks; other distribution systems such as donkey carts – where vendors play an important role – are not taken into consideration or viewed as an important part of the chain.

In the central areas of Khartoum the average consumption per person per day is reported (by KSWC) to be around 200 litres/day (equivalent to the European Standard consumption per person per day). The average for rural Khartoum State is estimated at 50 litres/day.

3.7   Greater Khartoum City sub-sector map

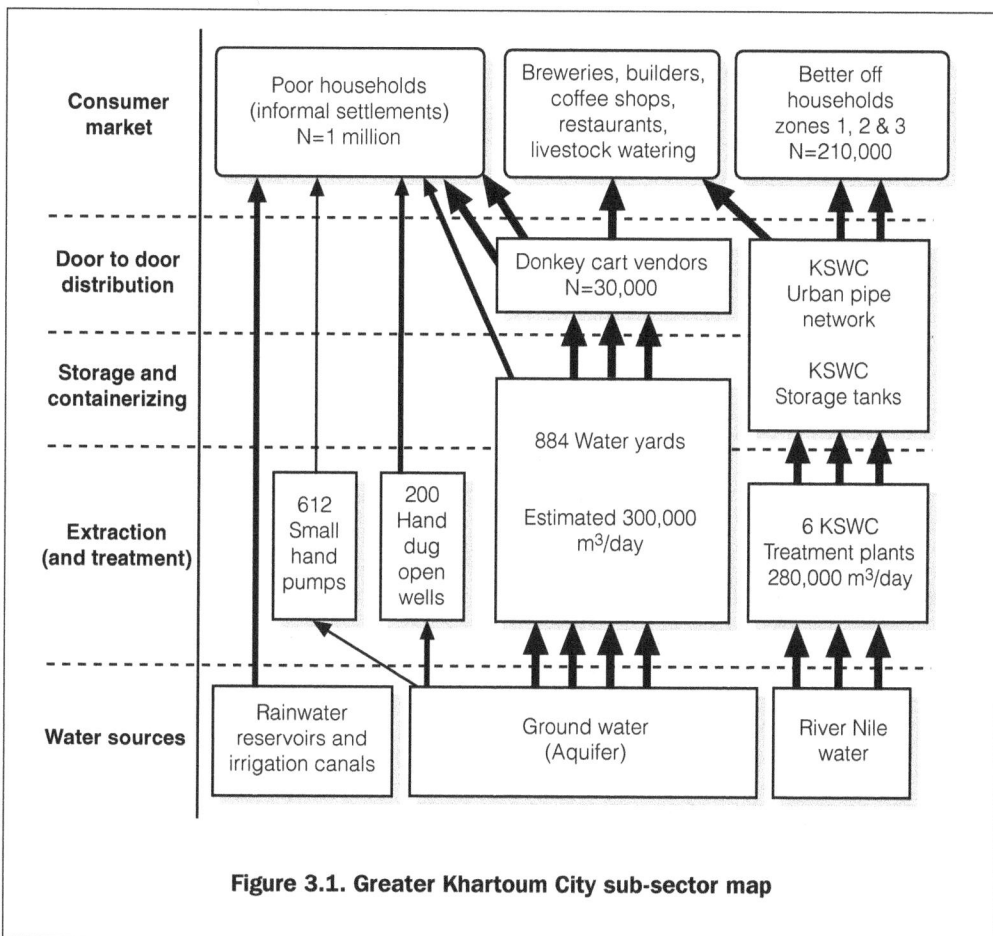

Figure 3.1. Greater Khartoum City sub-sector map

3.8   Current water policy issues

In 2002 there was a major policy change. The management role at community level was given to CBOs, mainly the Popular Committees. KSWC's terms were that the PCs should assume full responsibility for operation and maintenance costs, while the net revenue would be equally divided between the facility (i.e. the water-yard owned by KSWC) and the PC. Part of the PC's share of the water revenue is spent on other community services, such as basic education and health services. KSWC maintains its supervisory role over the management of the water facility.

Out of the PC management experiences other forms of partnership around water facility management evolved:

- Water facility directly managed by the KSWC

- Joint management by the KSWC and PC

- Management delegated by KSWC to Popular Committee, who form a water committee to manage the facility at community level

- Management by the private sector, whereby water revenue is divided equally between the NWC, which owns the facility, and the private sector management company

These four types of management were evaluated by KSWC's senior management and others in a workshop hosted by ITDG (Practical Action). The ITDG (Practical Action) field researcher for the 'Better Access to Water' project facilitated the meeting. The advantages and disadvantages of each of the four options are presented in Table 3.1 below. There may be a problem where third parties (NGO/ Private) are responsible for maintenance, but not repairs and replacement. There is little incentive for these organizations to carry out maintenance properly.

Partnership between KSWC and private operators

The horizontal expansion of Khartoum's informal settlements and the inability of the state government to effectively manage the water supply system in these settlements, led to partnerships with the private sector. Contractual agreements were signed with qualified firms (they needed to deposit collateral of SD1 million and show technical capability certificates). The initial agreement is for one year and is renewed annually. Small-scale enterprises are given water-yards on the town's peripheries where there is a high population density and good conditions. If the water-yard needs to be renovated or the engines changed, KSWC and the business each contribute 50 per cent of total costs. People buy water from the water-yards, which are fitted with meters to measure the amount of water used. Revenues from sales of water at the water-yards are divided between the enterprise and utility in the ratio of 80:20. To avoid complications a flat-rate tariff is used, and the meter is read monthly by the utility (KSWC). This type of partnership started with only a few water-yards but there are now more than 20 others in the Dar Al Salam (Omdurman) informal settlements.

Table 3.1. Advantages and disadvantages of management options		
Management option	**Advantages**	**Disadvantages**
KSWC	Timely response to breakdowns	Labour-intensive and costly to operate Water hygiene is not adequate. In most cases yard operators have not received hygiene education. Not conducive to popular participation
KSWC with Popular Committee	Enables community to share management responsibility	Lack of transparency PC lacks experience and managerial skills
Popular Committee	Community shoulders management responsibility Enables community delegates to learn by doing Cheap because of voluntary work extended by members of the Popular Committee	Instability in the membership of the executive committee PC assumes mixed roles – political and development Lack of sense of accountability – especially with respect to maintenance Use of water revenue in non-water community services e.g. schools, health centres, etc. Promote hygiene measures Overexploitation of the water facility
NGO / CBOs and private sector agents	Responsive to the interests and priorities of the target population Lobby government for community support Hold government accountable to poorer sector of the population Private sector participation induces strong element of financial sustainability	Lack of transparency regarding facility ownership and roles of other stakeholders NGOs create dependency among served population by extending free services Option to hand over to CBOs at the end of the project period Though claims to be building the capacity of the targeted CBOs, very little has been invested yet

Most relevant to this research

- Priority is to rehabilitate old water distribution networks

- Encourage private sector participation and investment in water projects

- Link water and sanitation, especially in poor settlements

- Co-ordinate water source management between NWC, state water corporations (SWCs), and local authorities (Mahaliat)
- Encourage collaboration between NWC, local authorities and Popular Committees in resource management
- Extend piped water network to town's peripheries
- Implement a replacement policy
- Review the water tariff and the basis for water fees collection and use of water income in the operation and maintenance of the water facilities

Other guiding policies relevant to the research

- Modernize technologies used in the rural water development projects
- Invest in water resource studies and research
- Invest in manufacturing of water technologies
- Link water provision with environmental health education
- Train technical staff
- Invest in developing new water plants
- Use water harvesting techniques in rural areas
- Establish management information system
- Establish water development funds

Funding policy

- Provide funds for project execution
- Support and encourage the private sector to invest in water projects
- Encourage popular participation and material contribution in establishment of water supply systems
- Market sound water projects to foreign funding institutions

General policy for sanitation and environmental health

The goal is to extend the sanitation and environmental health services throughout the country with the specific objectives to:

- Help install a pit latrine for every household

- Help establish a health committee for every 2000 households nationwide

- Train a health promoter for every 400 people

- Establish eight pit latrines for every basic school and five for every secondary school

- Establish 25 pit latrines in marketplaces where daily visitors exceed 10,000 people

Guiding policy for environmental health promotion

- Expand water and environmental sanitation projects, especially in poor settlements where diarrhoeal infections are common. Improve water hygiene by chlorinating, washing donkey carts, and draining wastewater and stagnant water.

- Promote environmental health education to help counter problems related to traditions, habits and culture.

- Link water with environmental sanitation.

Chapter 4

Informal Urban Settlements in Khartoum

4.1 Informal settlements overview

The key characteristics of the different types of informal settlements in Khartoum are summarized in Table 4.1:

Table 4.1. Summary of types of informal settlement in Khartoum	
Type of settlement	**Characteristics**
Spontaneous	Illegal unplanned settlement Houses are built from mud bricks and local materials Residents are mostly IDPs and poor rural–urban migrants Not entitled to water connection Could be demolished by the authorities
IDP camps	Recognized, allocated by the authorities, but not permanent Houses are built from mud and local materials, and plastic sheets Residents are mainly refugees from war and drought Basic services are provided mainly by humanitarian agencies (NGOs) Main water supplies are water-yards and handpumps High level of poverty
Informal settlements	Planned or permanent, not subject to removal Entitled to land tenure rights Entitled to social services by the state Houses are built from mud and bricks Not connected to piped water distribution networks Most depend on water-yard system Water distribution at household level is mainly via water vendors using donkey carts Social infrastructure is poor Residents are poor
Formal residential areas	Include Class 1, 2 and 3 planned residential areas Houses are built from bricks, mud, and local materials Social infrastructure more developed than in other settlements Households may be connected to piped water distribution networks

Land tenure: The 1970 land registration legislation specified that all lands for which there is no registered title are government-owned land. This was the basis for regulating land tenure in Sudan, including in Khartoum state. Accordingly, there are three types of land tenure:

i.   Leaseholds (77 per cent) – Land is rented from the government, usually for 90 years.

ii.   Freeholds (3 per cent) – The owner enjoys full title to the land.

iii.   Squatters (20 per cent) – The user is not entitled to the land and could be moved without compensation.

Informal settlements fall into the third category, and include shantytowns, spontaneous settlements, legal but unplanned IDP camps, and planned IDP settlements. The informal settlements share some common characteristics, including that:

• Settlers are the poorest people in the state. They have low incomes and lack basic services.

• Settlements are located on the periphery of urban areas, and have poor social and physical infrastructure.

• The population is originally from the rural areas, and they have been pushed out by the civil war and recurrent drought that has prevailed for almost three decades.

• Significant numbers of poor settlers from all over the country were pushed out by the escalating poverty which manifested itself in a lack of basic services and low incomes.

• They are ethnically and culturally diverse.

• They are areas where NGOs are likely to be active in providing assistance.

Everyone in the state capital, including in the informal settlements, is entitled to potable water for domestic household use, and KSWC is mandated to secure safe water for the whole population.

Many researchers agree that poverty is not only about income, but also incorporates access to basic services. Poverty is often characterized by high illiteracy, poor health, poor environmental conditions, and lack of basic needs. Research carried out in poor areas in Khartoum state showed that households rate potable water as their top priority, followed by access to employment, education, health, environmental sanitation, settlement upgrading, and security of land tenure.

During the past two decades IDPs and rural–urban migrants have drastically inflated the population of Khartoum state. The newcomers have created new settlements that extend deep into the rural villages. The new settlements also attract poor urban people who cannot afford the rent in the centre of town. These people are incorporated into the fabric of urban settlements by the support extended to them by the Ministry of Engineering Affairs through the land distribution scheme, which entitles them to a housing plot. This is carried out through one of two processes: treatment of spontaneous settlements or village treatment schemes. Both processes involve incorporation, re-planning or relocation. In 1990–97 200,000 poor households were allotted house plots, and in 1998–99 another 40,000 households were covered. Most of the land provided for house-building was fertile agricultural land, however. This is the case in places like Soba Al Aradi, Mayo Farms, Jebel Awlia, Dar Al Salam, and many other places. Water vendors serve 95 to 98 per cent of households in such communities.

4.2   Water services in informal settlements

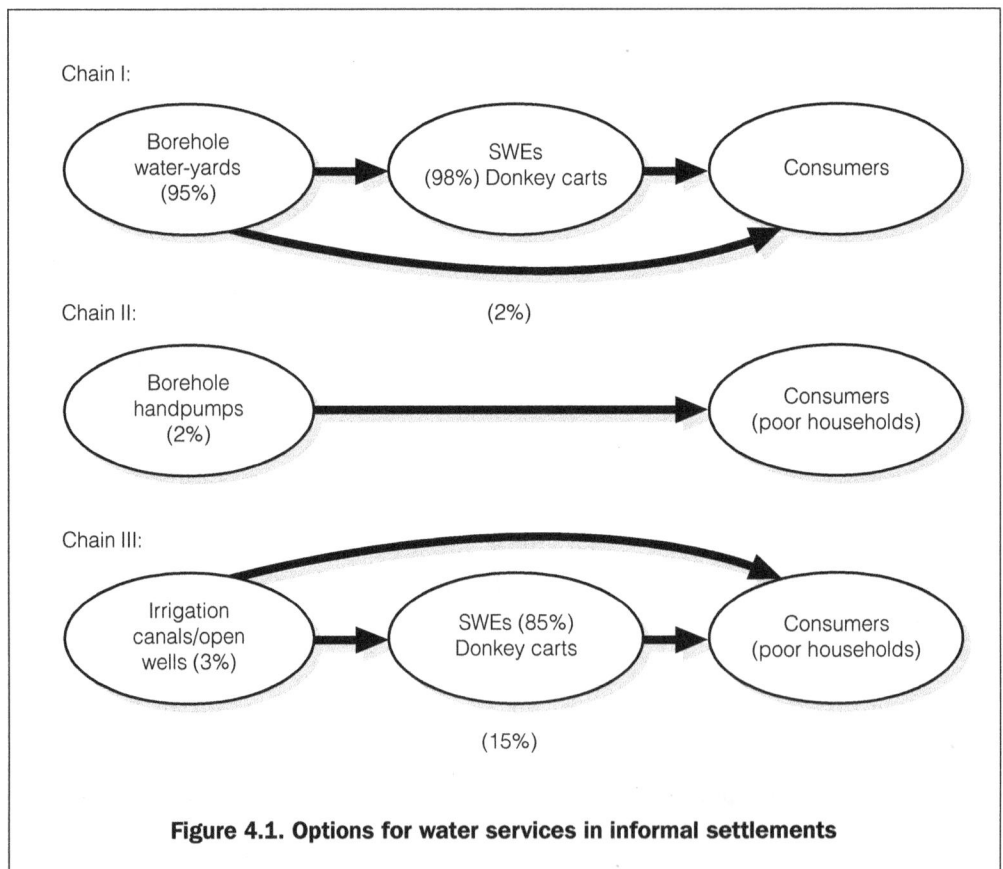

Figure 4.1. Options for water services in informal settlements

The different forms of water services include water-yards, handpumps, and open irrigation canals, with water vendors using water carts being the most important means of water distribution at household level.

Water supply systems for the poor

The type of water supply system used by poor people depends on the location of the informal settlement. Most are on the periphery and remote from the urban centre. These systems are the least developed and characterized by poor infrastructure. Few informal settlement households are connected to a piped system. The water supply systems also vary greatly; in Greater Khartoum nearly every site has a different system.

These include boreholes, handpumps, piped water, irrigation wells, open irrigation canals, surface reservoirs, and check dams. The piped water coverage is not great. For example in Girefat, Haj Yousif, While Nile, and Bugaa Omdurman South some 22 per cent of households have piped water and the rest (78 per cent) are not directly connected (UPAP, 2002).

Handpump systems are found mostly in IDP settlements, such as Al Salam Jebel Awlia and Mayo Farm, and have been installed by international NGOs to supply IDPs with water.

In Jebel Awlia (35 km south of Khartoum) people obtain water from both handpumps and water-yards.

NGO interventions in Khartoum State started with the provision of humanitarian assistance, providing relief food, shelter, and social services including water provision, health and sanitation. Then NGOs started to become interested in the livelihoods of the state's poorer communities. In the water sector in particular NGOs fund the construction of water facilities and train communities to manage them.

NGO interventions started with the destitute influxes of IDPs whose camps were initially set up without water supply systems (as in the case of Al Salam Omdurman). Potable water was trucked to the distribution points where individual IDP households queued and got their water directly from the water tankers or from the plastic reservoirs that water is stored in at the distribution centres. Gradually water-yards were installed by international NGOs like the Red Cross, such as in the district of Dawa Islameya, where management responsibility was shouldered by the Sudanese Red Crescent. Water stations are fitted with pipe outlets to facilitate easy water collection from the source.

In resettlement areas like Al Salam Jebel Awlia a number of international NGOs collaborated to establish water facilities, including MSF Holland, MSF France,

ADRA, Dawa, and others. A total of 172 handpumps were installed and four water-yards built.

Water, environmental health, and sanitation were popular and the concept of community participation manifested itself in the formation of Water Development Committees who were assigned the water management responsibilities and community mobilization functions. Community health promoters were trained and mobilized to educate ordinary citizens on water hygiene measures and public health. The youth were organized and trained in handpump repairs and maintenance. The Water Development Committee was created to provide day-to-day management of the four water-yards. Water Committee representatives were assigned for each block to supervise operation of the handpumps and assure proper use by beneficiaries. A spare parts stock for handpump repairs was established by MSF Holland to serve as a basis for a revolving fund to sustain repair and maintenance. It is assumed that beneficiaries replenish the used spare parts.

The average quantity of water consumed per capita per day for Dar Al Salam (as obtained from customers of four water facilities) are 23, 19, 21, and 21 litres. The maximum is 40 and the minimum 11 litres per capita per day. This confirms our research findings where during summer and winter the water consumption per capita per day is 25 litres while during autumn it is 16 litres. This data were obtained from 20 household interviews conducted by the research assistants.

However, as described in Section 3.8 (Current water policy issues) there are valuable experiences and lessons to be learned in relation to private sector participation and private public partnerships and water access for the poor.

4.3   Location selection

Two informal settlements, Soba Al Aradi (on the southern periphery of Al Khartoum) and Dar Al Salam (on the western periphery of Umm Durman), were selected as research sites based on the following criteria:

- They are planned and permanent and will not be abolished.

- They are poor low-income areas with poor social services.

- They are unlikely to be connected to the piped water system in the near future.

- Most households depend on water vendors for their water supplies.

- They are located on the peripheries of the cities.

The consultancy team, in collaboration with KSWC senior management, put together these criteria. As many communities share common characteristics, two sites rather than one were selected to enrich the research, as at Soba Al Aradi the water facility is owned and managed by KSWC while in most of Dar Al Salam the private sector manages KSWC-owned facilities. The communities share the characteristics above, plus:

- The communities were originally IDPs.

- Infrastructure in term of roads, schools and health services is very poor.

- They rely largely on water-yards for water supplies and the overwhelming majority are served by vendors.

- There is little formal sector employment.

- Most people are unskilled labourers or low-rank civil servants.

Chapter 5

Water Services and Poverty

5.1 Methodology

The methodology that was used included individual interviews and group discussions using checklists and observation. To identify interviewees at household level the customers of each of the 10 randomly selected SWEs were listed, and three households served by a particular SWE were selected based on varying distances from the water yard. Thus 30 households were identified and chosen for interview. Two gender-balanced teams conducted the household survey using a checklist.

5.2 Household income and water expenditure

The daily family food basket varies according to cash income. Sorghum (dura) is the main staple for most poor people. Beans, oil, sugar and seasonal vegetables are difficult to afford. Eggs and meat are rarely consumed because of the expense. Charcoal, wood and water take a significant portion of the household budget. Most households cannot afford to eat more than two meals a day. Some households reported only one meal a day (Elamin and Rabab, 2000).

Recent economic conditions have not only made it difficult for households to cover their daily expenses, but also limited the generosity culture at social gatherings. Other expenses including school fees, transport, and clothing are increasing rapidly and most households stated that they only buy their children clothes for religious occasions (Eid Fatar, Christmas, Big Bram 'Eid Kabeer'), and even then it is usually second-hand.

Medical treatment is sought only in emergencies. Borrowing from relatives or friends to buy medicines or getting free medicine from NGO health centres are the only options. Average and minimum income per month are SD12,000 and SD6,000 respectively.

Research carried out by the Urban Upgrading and Poverty Alleviation Project (UPAP, 2002) showed that 35 per cent of households suffer from lack of job opportunities and that the main occupations of those working are unskilled labour

(53.6 per cent), petty trading (13 per cent), employees (18.8 per cent), artisans/ handcraft (11.6 per cent). Most labour opportunities are casual with an irregular and fluctuating low income.

Most people in poor settlements work in the informal sector. Few jobs are regular. The main occupations include skilled and unskilled labour. Skilled labour includes blacksmiths, welders, metalworkers, carpenters, mechanics, electricians, builders and others. Unskilled labour covers water vendors, and casual labour in housing construction and concrete works. A few residents work as low-ranking government employees, such as guards, cleaners, messengers, gardeners and other miscellaneous jobs. Women mostly work as tea sellers, petty traders, food processors, vegetable sellers, and as farm labour on neighbouring farms (including poultry farms).

Poverty statistics for the state capital are controversial. Between 70 and 95 per cent of people qualify as poor on the basis of earning US$2 or less per capita per day. Underlying causes of poverty are civil strife, drought, wider displacements, rural–urban migration, structural adjustment and the lifting of subsidies, problems related to alleged human rights issues and economic embargoes, and the destruction of basic social infrastructure such as potable water, health and education services.

The current monthly water rates (since 1995) per 'rural' household are SD150/ month. This was based on the 1995 flat rate water charge in third class settlements. Households typically pay about forty times this amount (i.e. about SD6,000/month) to buy water from vendors.

Dar Al Salam household information:

- Average household size is seven people.

- Female/male ratio is 52:48.

- 41 per cent of men are illiterate, along with 49 per cent of women.

- The school dropout rate for boys is 48 per cent, for girls it is 52 per cent.

- Average monthly income for 86 per cent of male-headed households is less than SD20,000.

- For male-headed households expenditure on food and non-food items is SD15,390 and SD7,700 respectively. The average household expenditure on water is about 9.2 per cent of total monthly income (author's research findings).

- For female-headed households expenditure on food and non-food items is SD14,400 and SD5,460 respectively.

- Expenditure for an average household is SD22,893, while their income is only SD12,336. The expenditure:income gap is 46 per cent, and is sometimes met by remittances and donations.

- 80 per cent of respondents reported incidences of water-borne disease. 20 per cent reported bilharzia infections, reportedly caught when respondents were working on the Gazera irrigation scheme.

- People reported that since the water-yard was handed over to the private company there has not been a breakdown.

A water-yard consists of an enclosure containing a borehole and overhead storage tank. Groundwater is pumped to the storage tank, and people come to the water-yard to collect water supplied by pipe from the storage tank. Respondents reported that when the water-yard breaks down vendors bring water from far away. In such cases the price for two jerrycans increases from SD25 to SD30. In response households automatically reduce their water consumption to keep expenditure low. Many people reported a reduction in the number of baths, and washing clothes is kept to a minimum. This has negative effects on general sanitation for the household members. The water rate for urban households (formal settlements) directly connected to the piped water distribution network is SD1,000, SD2,000 and SD4,000 per month for Class 1, Class 2 and Class 3 areas respectively. This water charge is low compared to an average rural household's monthly expenditure on water (SD6,000). The latter mainly get their water from water-yards via vendors.

In very poor settlements the average household would spend between 17 and 25 per cent of its income on water for domestic use (Omer, 2002). Other sources show figures of between 9.3 (our research findings) and 30 per cent (Elamin and Rabab, 2000) of total household income spent on water.

- To solve water shortage problems people suggest that more water-yards be created, that piped networks are installed, and that water storage facilities are improved.

- Although consumers complain about high water prices, they appreciate the service provided by vendors. Some mentioned that during crisis periods vendors continue to supply customers with water and give them a grace period to pay. For good clients this could be up to one week.

- Some 95 to 98 per cent of households in Dar al Salam get their water from vendors.

- Households pay a maximum of SD6,000, which is about six times the price paid by those with piped water in the third class residential areas.

- Poorer households within a reasonable walking distance from a water-yard obtain water directly from the source. In such a cases water is sold at SD5 per jerrycan, and most women and children who fetch water using plastic jerrycans, typically of 16-litre capacity. Some women and children who collect water are considered to be too poor to pay for water, and the operator does not charge these people.

Household budgets

According to the field survey results from Dar Al Salam average household water expenditure is SD3,650, while average household income is about SD39,300. This means water expenditure accounts for 9.2 per cent of total household income. A survey conducted in the same area in April 2002 (Omer, 2002) showed that average household expenditure on water in four sites was 25 per cent, 17 per cent, 11 per cent, and 12 per cent of total household income.

Table 5.1.   Rough breakdown of household budgets

HH #	Food	Water	Clothes	Medication	Education	Travel	Social events	Others (electricity)	Total expenditure	Estimated income
1	15000	3000	-	2000	600	1000	1000	-	22600	30, 000
2	45000	3000	1000	5000	7200	-	5000	2000	68200	45,000
3	15000	3000	-	3000	3700	900	-	-	23900	22,000
4	36000	3500	2000	1000	900	-	1000	1000	45400	100,000
5	15000	1500	-	-	1000	2400	200	800	20900	21,000
6	30000	4500	-	-	1000	700	1000	-	37200	30,000
7	30000	4500	-	4000	-	5000	-	-	43500	50,000
8	45000	6000	-	3000	15000	800	-	-	69800	70,000
9	21000	4500	-	3000	1500	-	-	-	30000	30,000
10	30000	3000	1800	-	600	-	300	-	35700	25,000
Total	282000	36500	4800	19000	31500	10800	7500	3800	397200	393,000
%	70.9%	9.2%	1.2%	4.8%	7.9%	2.7%	1.9%	0.9%	100%	
Monthly average	28200	3650	480	1900	3150	1080	750	380	39720	

Source: Omer (2002)

Table 5.2. Average household water consumption for Dar Al Salam (Umm Durman)			
SWE No.	Winter	Summer	Autumn
Quantity in jerrycans/HH/month			
1	240	240	240
2	300	300	300
3	240	240	180
4	360	240	160
5	120	120	120
6	480	360	240
7	360	360	360
8	480	480	480
9	360	240	120
10	240	240	120
Total	3180	2820	2320
Average/HHL/month	318	282	232

Source: Author's field survey, Dar Al Salam, March/April 2004

From the table above:

a) Water consumption per capita per day during the summer (from mid-April to the end of June) is as follows:

1) Average water consumption per HH per month in litres (318 jerrycans @ 16 litres/jerrycan) = 5,088 litres

2) Average water consumption per HH per day (5,088 litres/30 days) = 170 litres

3) Average water cost per HH per day (170 litres at SD25 for 32 litres) = SD133

4) Average water consumption per person per day (170/7) = 24 litres

b)   Water consumption per capita per day during the winter (from October to mid-April) is as follows:

1)   Average water consumption per HH per month in litres (282 jerrycans @ 16 litres/jerrycan) = 4,512 litres

2)   Average water consumption per HH per day (4,512 litres/30 days) = 150 litres

3)   Average water cost per HH per day (150 litres at SD30 for 32 litres) = SD141

4)   Average water consumption per person per day (150/7) = 21 litres

c)   Water consumption per capita per day during the autumn (from July to September) is as follows:

1)   Average water consumption per HH per month in litres (232 jerrycans @ 16 litres/jerrycan) = 3,712 litres

2)   Average water consumption per HH per day (3,712 litres/30 days) = 124 litres

3)   Average water cost per HH per day is as for summer and winter, between about SD135 and SD140

4)   Average water consumption per person per day (150/7) = 18 litres

Note: Average household size is 7 people.

From these calculations it is clear that water consumption per capita varies slightly with the season. The highest consumption is during the summer when the temperature is relatively high, followed by winter and autumn is with the lowest consumption. The reduction in water consumption during autumn is attributed to the increase in the cost of water, when two jerrycans increase from SD25 to SD30. Households resort to reducing water consumption.

The field survey results are quite similar to the results in Table 5.3 from a previous survey in 2002:

Table 5.3. Household water consumption in April 2002			
Water-yard	**Water consumption (litres/capita/day)**		
	Maximum	Minimum	Average
Number 42	30	18	23
Number 32	30	11	19
Number 43	34	12	21
Number 27+ associated blocks	40	7	21

Source: Omer, 2002

Consumers:

a) *Water for domestic household use*

Our findings from Dar Al Salam (April 2004) showed average water consumption per household per day to be 170 litres (summer),150 litres (winter) and 124 (autumn). These figures are comparable with figures obtained from same settlement in April 2002 (see Table 5.3).

b) *House construction*

As houses in Dar al Salam are built of mud and mud bricks, this creates high water demand.

c) *Enterprise*

Consumers also include owners of small businesses such as restaurants, tea sellers, beer makers, and dairy farms.

d) The distance from households to the water-yards is between 50 and 750 metres. On average 377 donkey carts are served by the water-yard each day (between 140 and 611 per day). This means 377 carts each making four visits per day, or about 1,500 cart loads.

About 180 jerrycans of water are collected by individuals directly from the water-yard each day, 85 per cent by females and 15 per cent by males.

Water use in informal settlements

Domestic water uses include drinking, cooking, washing clothes, bathing, and watering a few animals or chickens.

Water uses by businesses include:

- brick making;

- house building;

- restaurants;

- tea sellers;

- local beer brewers; and

- truck owners serving animal traders.

5.4 Coping strategies

The poor households within walking distance of the water-yard normally get their water free, directly from the source. Others economize on water use. On average household daily water needs range from 6 to 12 16-litre jerrycans (100–200 litres in total). Individual jerrycans are filled for SD12.5 (SD0.8 per litres). A full donkey cart load (350 litres) sells for SD250–300.

Poorer households buy cheaper, poor-quality water, which is obtained from salty wells, irrigation pumps and open irrigation canals (depending on location). Some households resort to limiting their water use, which is reflected in poor sanitation and hygiene, which has negative impacts on people's health. In all places water consumes a significant part of household income.

Our field research indicated that in cases of water shortage due to breakdown of the facility water prices increased by 150 per cent. Household consumption decreased drastically (by 54 per cent) as households restricted their water use to drinking, cooking and washing dishes. This directly negatively affects other uses such as hygiene, laundry, house cleaning, and other sanitary measures. Although there is no data from the health institutions, water-related diseases such as diarrhoea and eye and skin infections are quite common in poor communities that suffer from acute water shortages. Another coping mechanism that poor community members resort to is using unsafe water sources like open irrigation canals, water pools and shallow open wells.

The three old water treatment stations need rehabilitation. Most of the pipe network is obsolete (designed in the 1950s) and needs rehabilitation. Leakages are common, which leads to water contamination and water ponds, which provide good breeding habitats for mosquitoes, who transmit malaria, and for other water-borne diseases like bilharzia.

Chapter 6

Small Water Enterprises (SWEs)

6.1 Methodology

The methodology followed included interviews with individual SWEs selected at random: ten from Dar Al Salaam community, and ten from each of three water yards in Soba Al Aradi. Thus 40 SWEs were interviewed in total.

6.2 Overview of SWEs

The main water supply for informal settlements is the water-yard system. Borehole water is pumped from an underground aquifer 300–500 feet deep. Submersible electric pumps or mechanical pumps are used to pump the water into an elevated tank. The tank is connected to standpipes from which donkey carts or individual's jerrycans are filled. Water vendors use donkey carts to transport water to sell directly to households. These carts cover between 95 and 98 per cent of water distribution at household level, while 2 to 5 per cent of households (mainly women and children) fetch water directly from the source.

Both water vendors and consumers live in similar circumstances. The informal settlements are characterized by lack of access to income and basic services (health, water, education, markets, roads, and others).

Water vending using donkey carts fitted with barrels is quite a popular job in informal settlements that have no piped water. It is also practised in formal settlements with piped connection when there is a prolonged lack of electricity or mechanical faults in their pumping station.

Water access via vendors

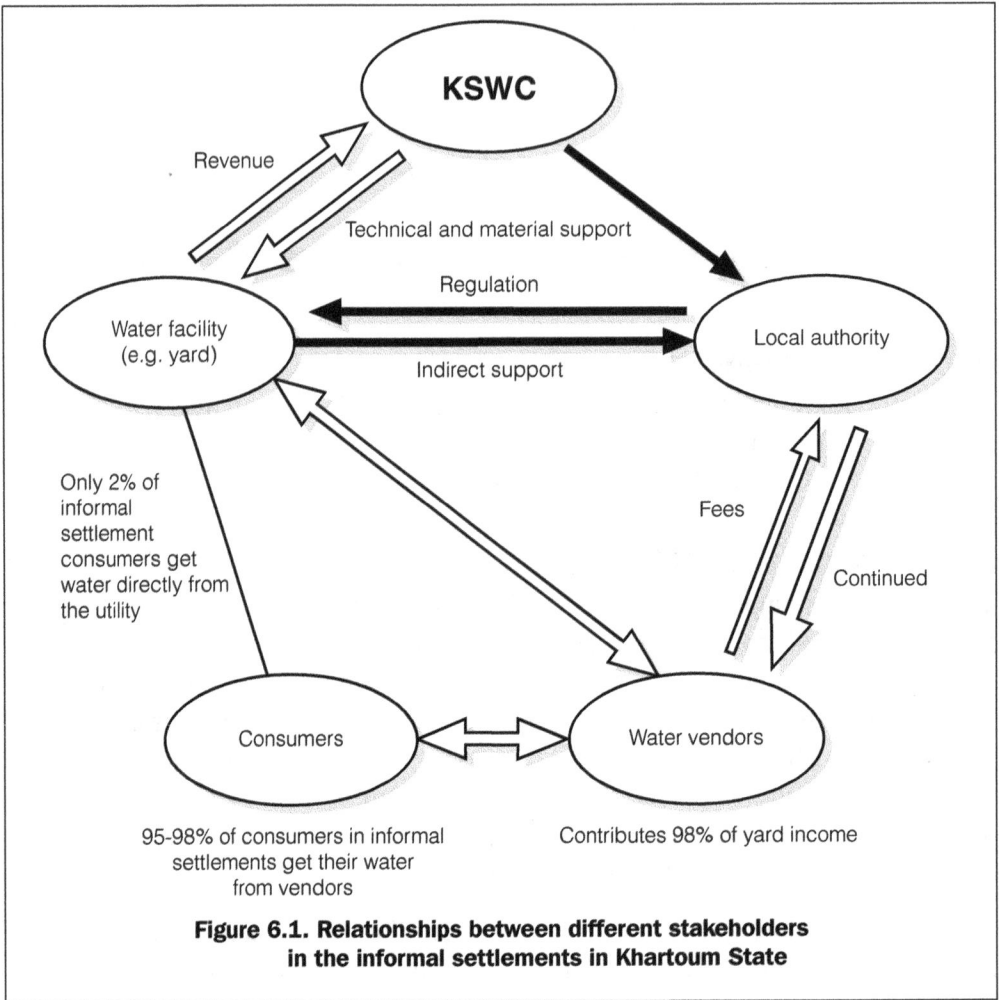

KSWC

Revenue

Technical and material support

Regulation

Water facility
(e.g. yard)

Indirect support

Local authority

Only 2% of
informal
settlement
consumers get
water directly from
the utility

Fees

Continued

Consumers

Water vendors

95-98% of consumers in informal
settlements get their water
from vendors

Contributes 98% of yard income

**Figure 6.1. Relationships between different stakeholders
in the informal settlements in Khartoum State**

Figure 6.1 summarizes the situation that exists in almost all informal settlements in Khartoum State. (It is meant to be qualitative but some numbers are included.)

Vendors play the central role in water distribution to poor households in the unconnected settlements. The total population served by vendors in Greater Khartoum is about 2,450,000 people. Almost all the water vendors use donkey carts for water distribution.

Vendors have a strong direct but informal link with the facility where they buy water. The facilities recognize the importance of the vendors, but are not responsive to their complaints about the increased water rate (which is fixed by KSWC at central level).

An NGO (ACF) intervention in Dar Al Salam local authority in Omdurman town that covered blocks 42,43, 23, and 27 gave the following financial information (see Table 6.1):

Table 6.1.	Water revenue and expenditure from four water-yards in Omdurman town				
Water-yard	Water revenue (SD)			Expenditure	Balance
	Donkey carts	Jerrycans	Total		
Number 42	90,000	0.0	90,000	42,000	48,000
Number 43	915,750	19,800	935,555	525,200	410,350
Number 23	713,000	13,050	726,050	442,260	283,450
Number 27	521,500	89,250	530,400	490,000	124,470

Source: (Omer, 2002)

As Table 6.1 shows, 98 per cent of revenue is generated from sales to donkey cart vendors, and only about 2 per cent from direct consumer purchase. This proves the feasibility of water distribution through the use of donkey carts in remote areas where extending the pipeline would be too expensive.

According to an ACF evaluation report conducted for eight water-yards in Dar Al Salam (Hamid), the population served by a water-yard ranges from 400 to 770 households, depending on the location. The average number of household served by an average yard is 575 households.

The average number of donkey carts served by a water-yard per day is 377 carts. The carts carry 384 litres of water and visit the yard on average four times a day. (These figures were obtained from eight water-yards in Dar Al Salam by directly recording the number of carts that attended the water-yards each day.)

Vendors have a strong direct but informal link with their customers. Consumers are not happy about water price increases dictated by operators of the water-yards, and this negatively affects the relationship between the vendors and consumers. In most cases it is the vendors who lose from water rate increases for a short initial period, but afterwards consumers bear the additional cost.

The bulk of households do not live near the water-yard and do not have a direct link with the operators as they buy their water from vendors. The poorest households, especially those close to the water-yard, may get free water directly from the source.

The local authority plays both a policymaking and a regulatory role for both water-yards and vendors. The health section of the local authority is supposed to monitor the hygiene situation of the water-yard and its surroundings, to inspect the water carts, and to inspect the donkeys' and vendors' health. The local authority also checks on validity of licences and health cards and imposes fines on defaulters. It seems that the local authority is more interested in the vendors as a source of income rather than as important actors in water distribution to household level.

The relationship between the local authority and the vendors is 'top down' and is seen by vendors as exploitive and punishing. Vendors in the locations surveyed complain about the high fees to obtain licences, health certificates and work cards, which cost SD18,500 in Mayo Farm and SD7,500 in Soba Al Aradi. (The fee in Mayo Farm is much higher because of the high demand for water due to the presence of a big market.)

Annual licences

Individual Working Card (Health Permit)	2,000
Donkey Health Licence	1,300
Cart Licence	2,380
Vending Licence	12,500
Garbage Collection Tax	700
Total	SD18,780

The high water cost paid by rural households provokes a logical question related to water-yard efficiency, cost effectiveness and reliability. For the 80 per cent who are not connected to the piped distribution network, do KSWC and policymakers recognize the role played by SWEs in water distribution to households, especially to the poor? SWEs do not receive any kind of support from KSWC or other authorities or institutions to help them to deliver services to consumers. They are also over-taxed (this mainly refers to Department of Health officials – see the many different licences and taxes above).

Officials need to understand better the role of SWEs in order to help them to extend efficient, reliable services to those living in informal settlements. Questions related to small-scale enterprises regarding the working environment including political acceptance, legislation, licensing, taxation, access to credit, barriers to entry, registration, cartels, and the trading environment are felt to be important concerns to SWEs. Consumers' concerns and opinions focus on water quantity, quality, accessibility and affordability, convenience, reliability and trust.

6.3 Settlement sub-sector map

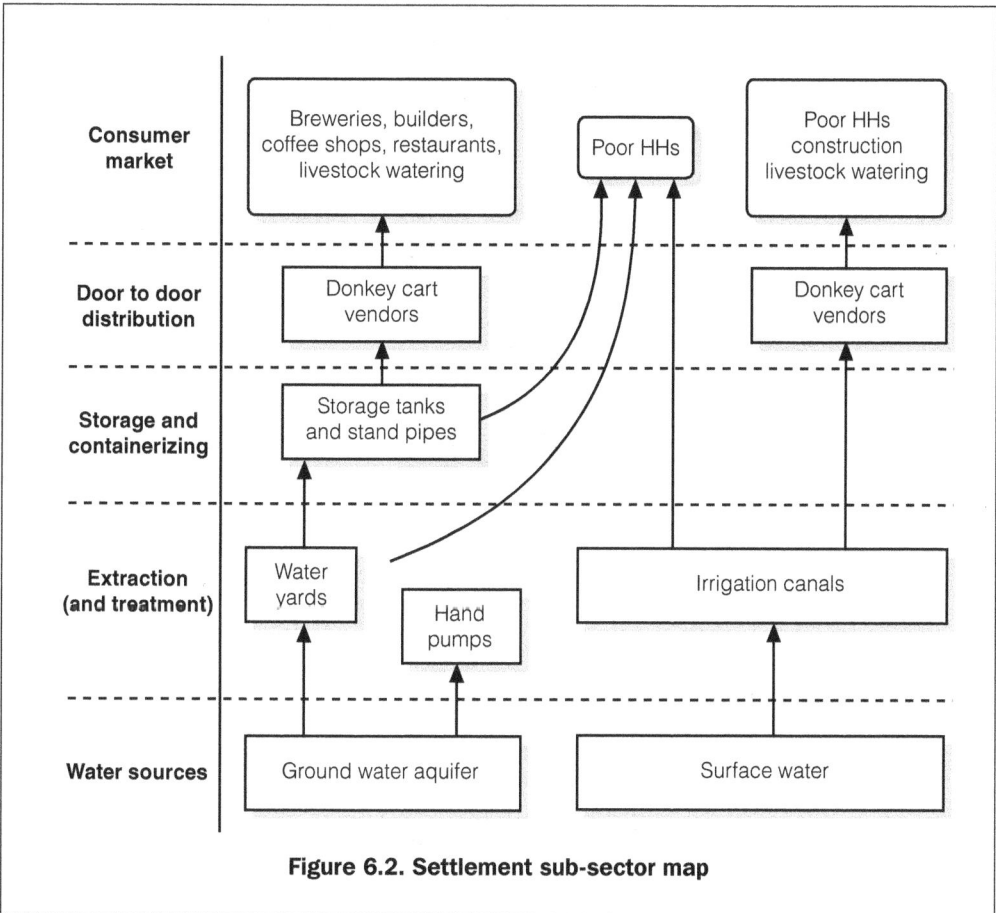

Figure 6.2. Settlement sub-sector map

6.4   Value chain

The pie chart in Figure 6.3 shows the components of the final cost to the consumer.

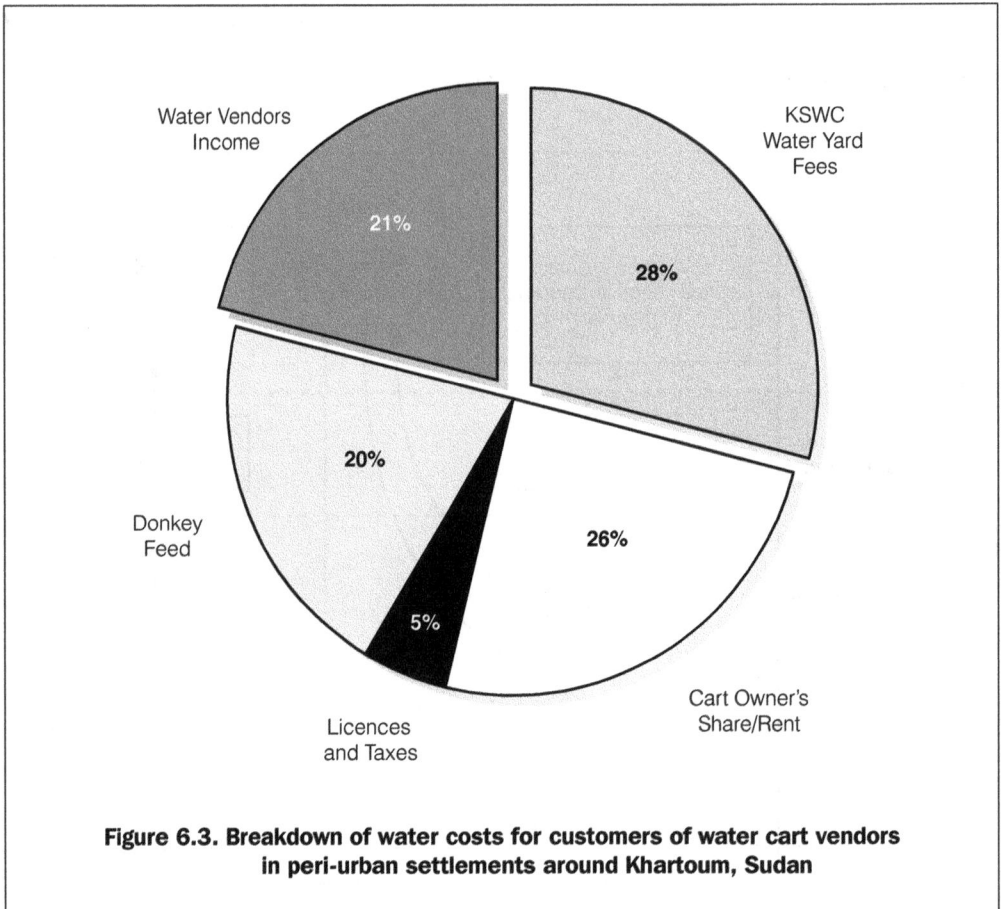

Water Vendors Income — 21%

KSWC Water Yard Fees — 28%

Donkey Feed — 20%

Licences and Taxes — 5%

Cart Owner's Share/Rent — 26%

Figure 6.3. Breakdown of water costs for customers of water cart vendors in peri-urban settlements around Khartoum, Sudan

6.5   Livelihoods of SWE operators

All water vendors belong to the poorer sectors of the communities they serve. In new informal settlements water vending constitutes a good business for local entrepreneurs who can afford to invest in water carts. In Soba Al Aradi one person owns up to eight water carts, which are run by others, but this does not appear to be typical.

There is an informal agreement between the cart owner and the operator. After deducting the cost of the donkey feed, the net water sale revenue is divided equally between the cart and donkey-owner and the operator. Normally this partnership is broken when the operator is able to save enough money to buy his own cart and donkey and be independent.

In new settlements the demand for water is very high because everyone is building and water vending is a very rewarding business for vendors. In older settlements, however, domestic use predominates and water vending is less rewarding.

Therefore in old settlements, where house building is less active and demand for water is lower, many donkey cart owners rent out their carts to operators rather than getting into revenue-sharing arrangements. A flat monthly rate is fixed, depending on the type of barrels mounted on the donkey carts. Carts equipped with Mobil and Fox barrels are rented out at SD600 and SD500 per month respectively (the difference between Mobil and Fox barrels lies in the gauge and therefore the durability of the steel from which the barrels are constructed).The cart-owner normally supervises the use of the cart and the hirer provides food for the donkey.

A new water cart costs SD50,000 while a second-hand one costs from SD35,000 to SD40,000. A good donkey for pulling a water cart would cost about SD35,000. For capital assets worth SD70–80,000, a daily rental cost of SD500 is typical, and seems fair.

Some ambitious water retailers expressed an interest in moving out of water vending and instead operating donkey carts designed and used to transport local people. Some boys described the transport carts as a decent, entertaining and rewarding business. 'The transport cart driver is clean, smart and enjoys good customer relations and pleasant companionship.' This shows how dissatisfied some water vendors are with the kind of business they perform, as it is extremely physically arduous and has a low status.

The research conducted in Dar Al Salam and Soba Al Aradi analysed in detail the problems faced by SWEs, their roles and other related key issues.

The water vendors of Dar Al Salam community
Ten water vendors in Dar Al Salam were randomly selected and interviewed. The analysis indicated that most of them are between 12 and 16 years old. All of them are school dropouts who did not complete their basic education. They reported that they left school because of poverty, to support poor parents or earn their own income. They are the breadwinners in their households. The rest of the vendors (a minority) are adult males between 24 and 30 years old. This group is married and has children.

Some 80 per cent of Dar Al Salam vendors own their donkey carts; the other 20 per cent get them through profit sharing. Water cart filling time is between 30 and 60 minutes. Travel time to customers' houses varies from 5 to 30 minutes. Two jerrycans (16 litres per jerrycan) are sold for SD25 during summer and winter and for SD30 in autumn. (Water is more expensive in autumn because of the muddy and slippery paths.) Vendors reported that the water tariff is reasonable yet customers would not accept any increase in the water rate.

The water vendors of Soba Al Aradi

Thirty water vendors were interviewed. They were randomly selected from a list of those queuing at three neighbouring water-yards at the time of the field survey. The first water-yard is owned and managed by KSWC, the second was installed and is managed by the Sudan Red Crescent, and the third (originally established for farm irrigation) is owned and managed by a private farmer.

Most water vendors in Soba Al Aradi (83 per cent) are adult men between 18 and 35 years old, 40 per cent of whom are illiterate. The other vendors are children who are 16 or 17 years old. Overall, approximately 55 per cent are married with children, and approximately 45 per cent are not married. Almost all vendors are supporting their immediate family plus parents and younger sisters and brothers. The average household size is 6.3, but it ranges between one and 12 people per household.

Vendors visit the water-yard three to five times a day (on average four). A few reported visiting eight times a day. The maximum waiting time in the morning is 30-45 minutes; in the evening 30 minutes (Omer, 2002). Fifty per cent of vendors own their carts and donkeys. 30 per cent rent them, and the other 20 per cent are in profit-sharing arrangements.

All vendors interviewed feel that they are mistreated by the local authorities, who charge high fees for licences to work. Many taxes, such as garbage collection fees, health certificate fees and others are imposed on them (SD6,500 for licence and health certificate fees, and SD550 for waste disposal and others). Vendors think such fees are beyond their capacity to pay. Therefore their work is continuously disrupted by the authorities, who usually confiscate the carts until they pay. Many carts were observed in Mayo local authority premises during the field survey. Also, while conducting the field survey in Dar Al Salam researchers saw the water-yard almost empty of vendors, who disappeared with their donkey carts to avoid police raids and having their carts confiscated. Of course such aggression towards vendors not only jeopardizes their work and income but also severely affects the income generated by the utility, as 98 per cent of its income is from vendors. Other repercussions affect the poor consumer, whose access to water will be endangered due to acute water shortages and price increases. The vendors suggest that licence and tax fees should be collected in four instalments over four quarters of the year, and that they should be well planned so that vendors are able to pay.

The utility and constraints faced by the vendors

The main constraints faced by vendors as reported by the interviewees are:

- Frequent breakdown of the water-yard, which in the case of old plants occurs from one to three times a month (Omer, 2002) and stops supply for two to seven days a month. During such periods water supplies are affected and vendors move to the nearest operational water-yard. This creates scarcity and wastes the time of the vendors, who have to wait for a long time to fill their cart. Waiting time varies from 30 to 60 minutes, depending on the breakdown of other water-yards. Time wasted because of the inefficiency of the water-yard management drastically increases cart-filling time and reduces vendors' income. Our research findings show that an average vendor sells about five cartloads a day, quite close to the four carts a day reported by the ACF study (Omer, 2002).

- There are very few taps, adding further to delays and reducing the number of carts that can fill up at once, which directly affects vendors' income.

- The grounds of the water-yards are rough and uneven, making it difficult for vendors to use the service efficiently.

- Water drainage in many yards is poor, causing muddy areas at cart-filling points.

- The water-yard is not fenced, causing sanitary problems because dogs and other animals are roaming around.

- Vendors have not seriously considered the possibility of organizing themselves. They are preoccupied with their daily survival needs, and believe that no one would listen to their complaints. Vendors think that the authorities do not value their services, and are only interested in collecting tax from them.

- Travel time to the customers' houses varies between 5 and 30 minutes. Regardless of travel time, customers pay the same price, which is between SD1.56 and SD1.85 per litre, depending on the season.

- Average daily net income per vendor is estimated at SD700 (ranges between SD400 to SD1,000). Given that the average vendor supports about 6.5 members of his family this would make the per capita income about SD107 (US$0.40).

- In Soba Al Aradi the charge at the KSWC-managed water-yard is SD70 per cart (384 litres), while water from the Red Crescent and the private farm is sold to vendors for SD50. The latter two are clearly more attractive to vendors than the first one.

Case study

Mubarak Fadul, a 19-year-old who operates his own cart, reported that his daily gross income is SD1,600. After deducting the SD400 cost of donkey feed (comprising alfalfa (SD150), sorghum stalk (SD150), sorghum grain (SD50) and dates (SD50)) he has a net revenue of SD1,200.

Mubarak, like other vendors, starts work at 7am and continues until 11am, when he breaks to feed his donkey and have a rest. The evening's work starts at 3pm and ends at 6pm.

A group of eight vendors interviewed agreed that an average daily income is about SD700.

Another reported that how much one earns depends on the kind of relationships one develops with customers. The payment terms vary between immediate cash, or payment at the end of the day, the week or the month. The best customers for water vendors are reported to be households, traders, and small businesses. Brick manufacturers are the worst, along with some builders who either defer payments or default. It is possible for vendors to take legal action against consumers who default payment, but that question was not addressed by this research.

6.6   SWOT analysis

Vendors' ideas for improving their situation could be summarized as: affordable tax, efficiency of utility, credit provision to enable vendors to buy their own carts, and grace period for water payment to the utility to help extend the service to consumers.

Table 6.2. SWOT analysis	
Strengths	**Weaknesses**
Vendors' role acknowledged by water consumers Demand for water is inelastic in informal settlements Presence of an estimated 30,000 water vendors serving 30% of total urban population in the three cities	Low income Inability to pay fees No aspiration and vendors do not value their role Negative feelings and mistrust towards the authorities Lack of organizational capacity and too weak to fight for their cause Lack of credit support
Opportunities	**Threats**
KSWC lacks resources to install piped networks to distribute water in informal settlements High cost of establishing piped distribution networks High number of consumers in informal settlements Interested researchers who could link SWEs to potential sources of support KSWC has started to appreciate the role played by SWEs in water distribution	Local authorities not providing tangible services to SWEs Confiscation of vendors carts for fee defaulters About 50% of vendors do not own carts themselves and work for others Frequent breakdown of water-yards directly reduces income Vendors are not part of the decision-making chain

Chapter 7

Consumer Perspectives on SWEs

7.1 Methodology

Information on consumer perspectives is based on the interviews and group discussions described in Chapter 5. In addition, a group discussion was held with ten female heads of households, backed up by observation.

7.2 Information obtained

Consumers complain about water shortages and also about how crowded the water-yards are – which contributes to the breakdowns which have happened about four times a month in the past, especially during summer. In such cases vendors have to fetch water from further away. Most of the respondents had no suggestions for how to improve the situation. A few said that the situation could be improved by connecting the water-yard to individual houses. To help mitigate water shortages some consumers suggested building more water-yards in the area. To overcome the acute water shortages that result from water-yard breakdowns people reduce their consumption at the expense of household sanitation and personal hygiene, mainly because of cost. The consumers' views about vendors are very positive, especially when water is supplied to them on credit at times of financial difficulties. Consumers expressed shared concerns with vendors that the water-yard frequently breaks down and consequently a lot of time is wasted waiting to fill their water carts.

Interviewees' response to the question of water-borne diseases is that they are less common during the dry season. People reported that the water-yard frequently breaks down. In the case of yard breakdown vendors travel for up to 45 minutes to obtain water from the neighbouring farm or Al Salama settlement, which is 6km away from the village. In such case a price increase is inevitable, so they cope by reducing consumption. Peoples' suggestions for improving the situation are the same as in other areas: add more water points, improve storage capacity, and extend the piped water network to individual households. There have been some attempts where the private sector in the informal settlement was assigned to establish a piped water network connecting the water-yards to individual households in block 13 of Dar Al Salam. But as the water rate fixed by the enterprise was three times the rate of Class 3 areas fixed by the KSWC, that is SD3000 per month, consumers refused to pay it (even though they pay the vendors about SD6000 per month). The logic behind their refusal to pay is that they should be treated equally by KSWC, like Class 3 settlements. The outcome was that the private company pulled out and asked KSWC for compensation. Another firm was contracted to manage the water-yards and take over the network liability. This again resulted in conflict between the new firm and the consumers, who mostly resorted to water vendors. Consumers view vendors as good workers who provide a good service. However a few complain that most vendors are children who easily get ill-tempered and misbehave.

Chapter 8

Utility Perspectives on SWEs

8.1 Methodology

The methodology used included interviews, discussions and workshops.

An August 2003 workshop facilitated by Partners in Development Services analysed the acute social services problems in Khartoum State. The need to improve water services is cited as a top priority. The root causes hindering access to water and the workshop's potential solutions are given in Table 8.1.

Table 8.1. Root causes of poor access to water and potential solutions	
Root causes	**Solutions**
1. Water sources	
1.1. The water supply from treatment plants is inadequate.	1.1. Install additional water-pumping stations.
1.2. Borehole water supply is inadequate and has salinity problems.	1.2. Rehabilitate water sources.
1.3. Some of the water-yards are working below capacity.	1.3. Ensure steady electric power supply for the water-yard.
2. Poor piped network	
2.1. The piped network has a low capacity.	2.1. Rehabilitate the water distribution network.
2.2. The pipes are old and made of asbestos-cement.	2.2. Rehabilitate the water network.
2.3. Poor planning means network did not keep up with population increase.	2.3. Improve planning capacity.

(Table 8.1. continued on next page)

Table 8.1.	Root causes of poor access to water and potential solutions *(continued)*	
Root causes	**Solutions**
3. New town extension	
3.1. There are very few water pipes.	3.1. Increase Nile water supplies by building new station and additional piped connections.
3.2. They are dependent on water-yards.	3.2. Increase Nile water supplies by building new station.
3.3. There are few household water connections.	3.3. Provide more household connections.
4. Town's outskirts	
4.1. There are no water services.	4.1. Establish water-yards.
4.2. There are no water pipes.	4.2. Establish piped water network.
4.3. There is no planning.	4.3. Improve planning skills.
4.4. Water is polluted.	4.4. Introduce water sanitation.

In the above analysis the role of vendors in water distribution is not even mentioned; a piped network is the only solution proposed. In fact vendors were never even considered throughout the workshop, which focused on water supply systems and pipe distribution networks. It is relevant to recall the KSWC manager for rural water (Mr Al Tayeb Yagoub) who is part of this research team and who said 'Initially I did not appreciate the idea of focusing the research on vendors. Only after being part of this research did I start to realize the importance of vendors and the role they play in water distribution to households. Now in my fieldwork I am attracted by the vendors as key partners.'

8.2 Official perspectives on SWEs

Local authorities

The general health controls implemented by local authorities start with water source analysis and approvals for buying and selling drinking water. Officials from the local authority (Department of Health) assume a supervisory and quality control role from source to distribution networks, up to the household or end-users. They are supposed to carry out periodic inspections of water quality along the chain and take protective water treatment measures.

The local authority also supervises the sanitary conditions around the water points in the case of boreholes, ensuring that hygiene measures and protection against the spread of water-borne diseases are in place. Such measures include cleaning the area surrounding the source to keep it clean and clear of runoff water, animal dung and garbage, and treating the elevated water tanks and borehole water with chlorine against bacterial contamination.

The local authority decides on the water cart specification, design and hygiene conditions, for example that they have to be painted at least twice a year to prevent rust. The authority can also monitor the health of cart operators and their donkeys. It also supervises the personal hygiene of the cart operator. Based on the above conditions the local authority provides work licences to both the cart and operator. The cart driver also needs to have a work card to operate.

The local authority is responsible for developing a water resource map which shows water source by type by block to facilitate easy monitoring and control for both facility and vendors. In relation to the conditions of hygiene measures and licenses, the vendors interviewed were deeply concerned that the local authority often mistreats them.

Chapter 9

Consciousness Building

Workshop Output (Khartoum, 8 May, 2004)

The outcome of a shared analysis of the problems identified by stakeholders, including KSWC, vendors and consumers, is presented in Tables 9.1, 9.2 and 9.3.

Table 9.1.   Outcome of problem analysis. Problems faced by consumers
Debt, acute poverty and lack of permanent job
86% have incomes of less than SD20,000/month
Expenditure on water for domestic household use ranges from 9 to 25%
Very low quantity of water consumed per person because of cost – 11–24 litres per person per day – which threatens sanitation and health
For poverty reasons child labour and school dropout rates are very high. Children are important breadwinners in their households
There are some complaints about water being salty and of poor quality
Frequent water-yard breakdowns cause water price increases that are unaffordable to households

Table 9.2.　Outcome of problem analysis. Problems as seen by vendors
Increase in water tariff
Licences, health cards fees, waste fees, work card
Ministry of Health tax (SD3500)
Only 50% of vendors own donkey carts, 30% rent and 20% profit-share
Negative feelings and mistrust towards the authorities (locality)
Inefficiency of the water-yard and water deficits cause a lot of problems for the vendor
Inability to pay for the licence fees and being chased by the authorities that confiscate the carts
Vendors not organized and lack institutional capacity
Net daily income for an average vendor who owns his cart is estimated by vendors themselves to be SD700
For those who are renting carts daily their income is about SD500
And for vendors who profit-share with cart owners it is SD 350
Vendors reported that water vending does not help alleviate poverty at this level of income
Total number of vendors and carts in the state is estimated at 30,000. Water distribution via vendors covers 35% of the state's population in the urban and semi-urban settlements
Local authorities do not provide tangible services to the vendors

Table 9.3.　Outcome of problem analysis. Constraints as seen by KSWC	
Water station breakdown	Lack of spare parts, repairs and maintenance
Lack of connection networks	Tariff is high compared to irrigation farms
Lack of fencing	High cost of production
Water stagnation around the water points	Obsolete pipe networks
Shortage of technical cadre	

From the above analysis it is concluded that the water rate as fixed by the utility is relatively high, mainly due to KSWC's inefficiency in managing the water-yards, which in turn is due to shortages of qualified technical staff, spare parts, and tools, and the lack of funds. The increase in water rates is also attributed to relatively high taxes and fees levied by the authorities. Inefficiency is also evident in the time wasted by vendors sitting in long queues at water-yards, which is partly caused by the poor technology used (water carts).

The workshop provided an opportunity for different stakeholders to discuss the roles of SWEs, and raised awareness of the importance of SWEs for water supply in Khartoum.

References

Banaga, Sharaf El-Dean (2002) 'Final Report and Recommendations of the National Workshop on Internally Displaced Persons (IDPs)'. UNDP, Khartoum, Sudan.

Elamin, Mohamed and Rabab (2000) 'Base Line Survey'. IRC (International Rescue Committee), Khartoum, Sudan, May 2000.

KSWC (2002) *Khartoum State Water Corporation Report.* KSWC, Khartoum, October 2002.

NWC (1999) *Sudan National Water Policy*. Sudan National Water Corporation, Khartoum, September 1999.

NWC (2001) *The General Guiding Policies and Strategies for Drinking water Supplies*. Sudan National Water Corporation, Khartoum, November 2001.

Omer, Hamid (2002) *Household Survey.* ACF (Action Contre la Faim), Khartoum, Sudan, April 2002.

UPAP (2002) 'Urban Upgrading and Poverty Alleviation Project (UPAP)'. Unpublished report, Khartoum, Sudan.

www.ingramcontent.com/pod-product-compliance
Lightning Source LLC
Chambersburg PA
CBHW080254030426
42334CB00023BA/2820